...to The Ichthus File

We hope you enjoy it. Before you start, you'll need:

A BIBLE Get a readable version, like the NIV (New International Version)

A PEN It helps to write answers down, as well as things you want to remember or to pray for each day. Write in the File itself or in your own notebook.

A CLOCK Aim for 10-15 mins on each study at the start or end of your day. Don't get hung up if you miss a day- just get going again.

A BRAIN You'll have to think about the Bible passage and about how you might need to change. Think as you ask God to help you at the start of each study and when you pray at the end.

THE ICHTHUS FILE It's hip to be square! Yes, it is!

Isn't it -ism time?

How to use The Ichthus File

An optimist and a pessimist were brothers. On Christmas Eve, their parents filled the pessimist's room with loads of presents and the optimist's room with a big pile of horse manure. In the morning, the pessimist woke up and said: 'Oh dear, I'll never be able to open all of these.' The optimist woke up and said: 'Hmm, there must be a horse in here somewhere.'

Here's The Ichthus File, a series of Bible-reading notes that could just about be more exciting than a roomful of presents. If not, it certainly smells better than a pile of... exactly.

We asked those two brothers to look at The Ichthus File:

Oh dear, The Ichthus File looks rather long, doesn't it?
No! Not long enough! What a great way to open up the Bible!
Yeah, but why did they have to choose the book of Job?
Hey, I've always wanted to get my head round that book.
S'pose I'll start... but it all looks rather hard going.
Come off it! Graphics, questions, stuff to do, humour even.
Yeah, but it probably won't be very funny.

It's funnier than you being caught in a storm with no umbrella.
Oh, ha ha. Now what are those bits at the back of the File?
Oh, of course - Optional Extras! More in-depth, extra stuff.
Does that mean I have to do them as well?
No! The way you use The File is up to you. They recommend pretty regularly, even daily, but go at your own pace.
And are you going to tell me what those eye boxes mean?
No, but those nice guys at The Ichthus File will... you see, it's all designed to help you and me make progress with God.
The 'eyes' should help you as follows:

Please read the passage from the Bible.

Stop and think. Chew this stuff over. Don't hurry on.

Work out how these truths will affect you personally.

Pray: talk to God. Vital before and after each study.

Whether you're an optimist or pessimist, welcome to issue 8 of Ichthus File. More details about subs at the back. G'day!

MATT'S MATTERS

Matthew, part 2: The Introduction

Please meet Major Goof. Morning, Major!

We're sorry to say Major Goof first appeared - uninvited, we must add - in the last issue (no. 7). Did you notice him in the intro to Matthew's gospel? Page 3, column 2, paragraph 2, last line, to be precise.

We meant to write: 'The news of Jesus' rescue was now to go to all people.' But Major Goof snuck in and swapped 'now' with 'not'. Totally wrong. Nightmare. We can only apologise.

We need to warn you that Major Goof is back in this issue. Not, we hope, in causing disastrous spelling mistakes (we've told him off about that several times).

But we'll meet the Major as we dig into Matthew's gospel, part two. Our stride through chs. 8-18 will reveal several people who do a Major Goof with Jesus.

Some of the Jewish religious leaders refused to accept that Jesus' authority is that of God. That's a Major Goof for you.

The disciples kept mis-understanding who Jesus really is - and so failed to trust him in awkward situations. That's another evidence of the Major.

And some of the ultra-religious lot, the Pharisees, were outraged that Jesus mixed with society's rejects, those who were considered to be unfit for God. One more, Major.
But hold tight. Major Goof didn't trip everyone up: we'll meet a number of individuals who did acknowledge Jesus as he really is and threw themselves into following him.

Those are key people to watch in these chapters: Matthew's at pains to point out that, with the arrival of Jesus on earth, God's people would now be drawn from every class and nation. No longer any limits!

But watch for one last Major Goof: it's easy for us to assume we know about Jesus. Take a fresh look with us. And don't make the mistake of thinking you won't be surprised by what you find here.

That'll be all, Major: now clear off.

COR, CURE CARE
Matthew 8 v1-17

Remember the Sermon on the Mount (chs. 5-7)? Of course you do: Jesus' listeners being amazed at his authority, yeah? In chs. 8-9, Matt moves from Jesus' teaching to Jesus' deeds. Which were equally authoritative. Matt presents nine miracles, in three lots of three. After each lot comes another clip of action that Matt wants us to know about.

First, Jesus healed a man with leprosy, a Roman centurion and a woman. That really narked the Jews: how dare Jesus help people who shouldn't be allowed anywhere near God?

Read Matthew 8 v1-4.
LEPER LAUNDERED

v2: leprosy, a repulsive skin disease, was thought incurable. Lepers were banned from society: disgusting to look at, dangerous to get near (big health hazard), but even worse, were regarded as 'unclean', ie unfit for God (so coming into contact with one was held to make you 'unclean', too).

• But what do Jesus' words /actions reveal (v3)?

• What two things had this man realised about Jesus (v2)?

v4: odd? 'Don't tell anyone'? What would happen if he did?

• For what reason alone did Jesus want people to follow him? Instead, the healed man was to thank God at the temple.

Read v5-13.
SERVANT SAVED

The guy was a Gentile (a non-Jew), but see how Jesus describes his attitude and action (v10). Jesus is amazed.

• In what ways did the guy demonstrate faith (v5-6, 8-9)?

• Why was his faith greater than the leper's?

• What was the incredible result (v13)?

v11-12: ouch! Jews who thought they were 'in' with God were wrong: no, God's people would be from all nations, Jesus said. Jews who relied on their ancestry and not God would be kicked out from the banquet of heaven (v11).

• What's the only qualification for heaven (v10)?

Read v14-17.
MOTHER MENDED

Unique authority: many are brought, all are healed (v16).

• How does Matthew summarise all this (v17)?

• So what's he saying about the identity of Jesus here?

Tell Jesus your response to what you've taken in today.

For further study see the **OPTIONAL EXTRA** on page 56

NO COMPROMISE, PROMISE

Matthew 8 v18-22

When Jesus saw the crowd around him, did he:
a) sign autographs; b) preach to thousands; c) call for body-guards; d) heal all the sick?

When someone promised to follow Jesus, did he say:
a) 'Well done'; b) 'OK, let's go'; c) 'Hello and welcome to the bigtime'; d) 'Really? Wot, you?'

When a disciple had a family duty to keep, did Jesus say:
a) 'Sure, I'll wait around for a bit'; b) 'Yup, I believe in the family'; c) 'What, now?'; d) 'Oh well, if you must'?

None of the answers is right. Find out what really happened:

Read Matthew 8 v18-22.

Now give a right answer to the three questions above.

v18: surprise: Jesus avoided the crowds as they'd be liable to misunderstand his mission. He wasn't after hangers-on.

WATCH RASH PROMISES

See who the guy was and what he called Jesus (v19).
• *Was that description right? Think: was it enough?*

Jesus answered his promise with a severe warning:
• *What should the guy expect if he was to follow Jesus? Why?*
• *Why do you think Jesus answered like this?*

WATCH HALF-HEARTEDNESS

The second guy's different. See who he is (v21)?
Burying the dead (a son's job) had to be done within 24 hours.

• *Was his request unreasonable?*

• *What did Jesus say (v22)?*

It's fierce: 'Let the dead (ie, those with no spiritual life in them) take care of such matters.' The demands of Jesus not only take precedence. They do so immediately. Like now.

WATCH YOURSELF

Jesus stressed the constant insecurity of life as his disciple.
• *Why do we stupidly expect to have it differently?*

• *Are you like either of these two guys?*

a) ready to applaud Jesus and boldly promising to follow him?

b) got started as a disciple, then got distracted?

Jesus' demands are absolute and immediate: 'follow me'.
Will you? Watch what you say to him now...

POWER POINT
Matthew 8 v23 - 9 v8

'Roll up, folks, to see the world's first cherry-coloured cat! Amazing! Roll up!' etc. Bloke then appears with a black cat, says: 'So, it's a black cherry.' Umm. Chair-hurling riot follows. Jesus' miracles weren't tricks. The next three Matt gives us were proven. And they were pointers to who Jesus really is.

 **Read Matthew 8 v23-27.**
Power shower

Jesus was talking about what it meant to follow and trust him.
• *How did the disciples then respond when their trust was put to the test (v25)? See the contrast with Jesus (v24b)?*

Jesus challenged them (v26), then stopped the weather.
• *Had the disciples shown faith? Why was it 'little'?*

See their gobsmacked reaction (v27). Think what the miracle showed about Jesus. Who alone can control the weather?

 **Read v28-34.**
Demon hill

Spooky scene, v28. The demons (supernatural, evil spirits) knew Jesus' authority (v29), but continued to challenge it.
• *How was Jesus' miracle proved dramatically?*

The pigs' stampede and drowning showed the men they were cured. Think why the locals reacted as they did (v34).

Read ch. 9 v1-8.
Mat man

v2: bizarre statement, isn't it? The guy's paralysed - and there was Jesus telling him he was forgiven. Gee, thanks, mate.
• *But why was Jesus doing this? (v6 will help...)*
• *Why were Jesus' opponents outraged at what he'd said (v3)?*

Clever answer, v4-6: think which statement is easier to make.

Cracked it? It's easier to say: 'You're forgiven' 'cos no-one can prove it, right? But Jesus did the one miracle (the physical healing) to prove the other (his forgiveness). Wow!
• *What did this miracle show about Jesus?*

Sum up Jesus' authority from v23-27, v28-34, 9 v1-8.

Note the different reactions it provoked (v27, v34, 9 v8).
• *Were any right?*
• *What's yours?*

SPLOSH!

For further study see the **OPTIONAL EXTRA** on page 56

A RIGHT MEAL OF IT

Matthew 9 v9-17

Here's the second bit about Jesus between the second third and the third third of Jesus' miracles in chs. 8-9. Right? Er, think so.

Most of the action is at a meal-time: two lots of Jesus' opponents burst in to interrupt the main course. Jesus tucked into their questions with equal relish.

Read Matthew 9 v9-13.
Doctor on call

T-Cs were well-liked, respectable, patriotic civil servants. Not. Make that hated scum, known for extortion and corruption. Yet Jesus called Matt to follow (v9).
* *What does that teach us about Jesus?*
And Matthew didn't stop to think twice.
* *So what does that teach us about Jesus?*

Sharing a meal (v10) showed friendship: Jesus ate with those whom the religious Jews thought God had written off.
* *What was the attitude behind the Pharisees' question (v11)?*

Dig out what Jesus was saying in v12 about himself.
* *And what was he saying about the people around him?*

v13: Jesus wanted a change of heart, not external religion. He hadn't come for those who thought they were right with God but those prepared to admit their need of forgiveness. Ouch! Think what the Pharisees would have thought.

Read v14-17.
Bridegroom on hand

Then the disciples of John the Baptist marched in, all het up.
* *What did Jesus' answer reveal about himself?*
* *When would he be 'taken from them'?*

v16-17: Jesus drew a contrast with the Jewish religion.
* *Could they just add Jesus and his teaching to their rituals?*

* *In what ways was Jesus bringing something new?*

Sure, it was new: Jesus brought God's rule and his rescue. But it shouldn't have been unexpected: Jesus came (as Matt's told us) as the fulfilment of the Old Testament, on which the Jewish religion was based. The Jews should have seen that.

The meal time was about to be further interrupted. That's next. First, give answers from both halves of today's study to:
* *What do I need to face up to about Jesus?*
* *What do I need to face up to about myself?*

For further study see the OPTIONAL EXTRA on page 57

7

MEAL-TIME HEAL-TIME

Matthew 9 v18-34

Here's the third lot of three miracles which Matt's got for us in chs. 8-9. Only here, we get four - 'cos Jesus did one miracle en route to another. So Matthew includes it. Four for three! Boy, it was some meal-time Jesus was having. More interruptions now. He probably hadn't finished his main course...

Read Matthew 9 v18-26.
BE BACK FOR DESSERT

Catch the synagogue ruler's startling request: 'will you raise the dead, Jesus? No wonder his disciples went, too (v19). Drama on the way. The woman's bleeding made her 'unclean' under Old T law: no-one was to go near her or vice versa. Imagine 12 years like that... which is why she came up behind Jesus, rather than face-to-face, for fear of rejection.
• *What had she realised about Jesus - and not realised?*
• *What response did she discover (v22)?*
• *And what happened to her?*

Then, Jesus threw out the ruler's paid mourners (v23).
• *How could he say the girl was just 'asleep' (v24)?*
• *What extra does this miracle tell us about Jesus?*

v26: not surprising, huh?

Read v27-34.
GET THE COFFEE ON

Jesus tested the faith of the two blind men: they followed him all the way indoors (presumably back to Matthew's house) - then to be challenged by Jesus (v28).
• *How did Jesus respond to their trust in his power (v30)?*
• *Why did he warn them - sternly - to keep it quiet (v30b)?*

Still more action, with a man demon-possessed and dumb.
• *Was this double problem doubly difficult for Jesus (v33)?*

Finally, two reactions (v33-34):
The crowd: 'This is a world first. Nothing like this has ever happened among God's people before.'
The Pharisees: 'This can only be the work of the devil.'

Circle one word here which most describes your response:

Dismissive   Sceptical   Questioning   Indifferent
Impressed   Amazed   Thankful   Trusting

Tell Jesus, the same risen Lord, the reasons for your answer.

For further study see the OPTIONAL EXTRA on page 57

M PEOPLE

Matthew 9 v35 - 10 v15

A new phase in Matt's gospel now: Jesus, the one with unique authority in teaching (chs. 5-7) and miracles (chs. 8-9), hands that authority on to his disciples. They're sent out to do what Jesus has just done: a mission like his so far. As follows:

**Read Matthew 9 v35-38.**

THE MODEL

Matt gives another of his 'I'll-wrap-it-up-for-you' summaries.
- *What did Jesus' public ministry consist of (v35)?*
- *What were his motives (v36)?*

Think what the crowds needed to recognise about Jesus.
- *How are the crowds described? Isn't it true of people now?*
- *What was the great opportunity Jesus referred to (v38)?*
- *How should this make us act and pray, too?*

**Read ch. 10 v1-4.**

THE MEN

v2: 'apostles' means 'those sent out', ie the 12 disciples.
See what Jesus gave them (v1): incredible!
- *What would this enable them to do? Compare 9 v35.*

**Read v5-15.**

THE MISSION

Please complete their job description:

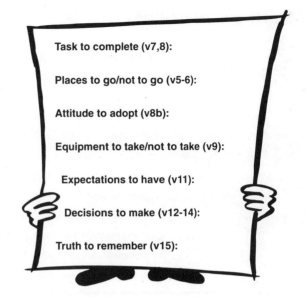

Task to complete (v7,8):

Places to go/not to go (v5-6):

Attitude to adopt (v8b):

Equipment to take/not to take (v9):

Expectations to have (v11):

Decisions to make (v12-14):

Truth to remember (v15):

The 12 were to go urgently (no luggage) first to the 'lost sheep' of Israel (v6): to warn God's people the Jews that king Jesus had come (v7) - and that failure to recognise his authority would be catastrophic for them on God's judgment day (v15).

Now consider how Jesus had been a perfect example of each piece of the job description above.

The 12 were to preach and do miracles. It's not the same for Christians now: we've a different, if related, job. That's given to us in Matthew 28 (the 'great commission'). See the OE!

For now, think how to pray for your friends or neighbours who don't know Jesus, using 9 v36-38 and 10 v15.

For further study see the **OPTIONAL EXTRA** on page 58

TAKING THE TROUBLE
Matthew 10 v16-31

Jesus next spelt out emphatically what doing his work would involve. And that spelling read C-O-N-F-L-I-C-T. Christians now mustn't expect otherwise. As we'll see, Jesus was speaking first about the 12's mission, but this passage clearly spells out the result of following Jesus in any age. We warn that some scenes may shock or offend misguided or unwilling disciples. Jesus made no apology. Nor do we.

Read Matthew 10 v16-20.
You

Jesus warned the 12 of Jewish opposition (v14). Now anybody (that's what the 'men' in v17 means) would oppose them. Picture how savage the conflict would be (v16a).
• *What forms could that opposition take (v17, 18, 19)?*
• *Would all this achieve anything (v18)?*

Later, Jesus gave orders to take his message to the world (Gentiles not just Jews). That task would begin with the 12. Note what commands Jesus gave his disciples here.

v19-20: Jesus promised that God's Spirit would equip these untaught disciples at times of great conflict. Yes, please!

Read v21-23.
have

• *What else would Jesus' mission lead to (v21, 22a, 23a)?*
• *How should Jesus' disciples respond (v22b, 23a, 23b)?*
v23: hmm, tricky: probably refers to the work of the 12 prior to the destruction of Jerusalem (Jesus' judgment) in AD70.

Read v24-25.
been

• *What should a Christian expect (v25)? Why (v24 too)?*

Read v26-31.
warned

Conflict ahead? It panicked the disciples all right (v26). But there's right and wrong fear, said Jesus. Describe each (v28).

Either a cowardly fear of people, or a sober respect for God. See what suffering Christians must also remember (v29-31)? God the terrible judge (v28) is not only all-knowing in intimate detail (v29-30), he's our loving heavenly father (v31).
• *Which of Jesus' warnings here do you need to remember?*
• *And which of his promises here?*

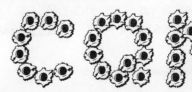

For further study see the **OPTIONAL EXTRA** on page 58

NO CON-CON CON
Matthew 10 v32-42

Conflict, part two: the rest of Jesus' teaching. Or we could say conflict-continued ('cos that's been the pattern for Jesus' followers ever since).

Get it straight: this is no con about the con-con. Jesus said the normal Christian life will generate conflict. We shouldn't go looking for it or stir it up - just know that Jesus' message always sparks opposition. No con.

Here, Jesus is holding up warning signs - lots of them (strong arms, obviously). Each symbol warns the casual Christian.

Read Matthew 10 v32-33.
Mouth

Spot the Christian's duty (v32a). And the result (v32b).
• *Why might we be tempted to do the opposite (v33)?*
• *When we're scared of standing up for Jesus, what two things should we remember (v31, v32-33)?*
• *What's a fate worse than human persecution (v33)?*

v32-33 show Jesus' role in God's final judgment. Big, huh?

Read v34-36.
Sword

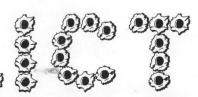

How could nice, inoffensive Jesus say that (v34)? Wasn't he about peace? Ultimately, yes: a peace with God through the cross. But he knew his message would first divide people.
• *What would be the regrettable result (v35-36)?*
• *How might a new Christian divide a non-Christian home?*

Read v37-39.
Cross

• *How important is Jesus (v37)?*
• *How important is he to you?*

v38: think how the disciples would later see this in action.
• *What was the lesson (and promise) for them - and us (v39)?*
• *What do you think 'losing our lives for his sake' means?*

Read v40-42.
Cup

The way we treat Christians is a test of our relationship with God. Those who welcomed the 12 into their homes (ie, accepted their teaching about Jesus) received God (v40). Wow.

• *Prepared to go on as a disciple of Jesus?*
• *What do you need to talk to God about from today's study?*

For further study see the **OPTIONAL EXTRA** on page 58

THE BAP CHAP
Matthew 11 v1-19

No introduction here. Just get on with it. Go on. Oh, please...

👀 **Read Matthew 11 v1.**

That verse neatly rounds off ch. 10.
So far... Jesus' rule - his kingdom - has been announced to the people of Israel by John the Bap (ch. 3), by Jesus himself (5-7), by his miracles (8-9) and by the apostles (10).
Now (chs. 11-12) we're shown how people were reacting to Jesus. First, it's The Bap's disciples who came to him...

👀 **Read v2-6.**
DISCIPLES DISCIPLED

As we'll see shortly, it's likely John was asking the question on behalf of his disciples: *they* were the ones confused.
• *What didn't they know (v3)?*
• *Why was this an important question?*
• *What did Jesus' answer tell them quite clearly (v4-5)?*

v6: Jesus knew people would take offence at him: after all, he didn't conform to their ideas much in what he said or did.
• *In v6, how does he encourage people to trust him?*

👀 **Read v7-19.**
QUESTIONERS QUESTIONED

Jesus in 'Now you mention it...' mode (v7).
• *What had the Jews rightly understood, says Jesus (v9a)?*
• *But what had they totally failed to see (v9b, 10, 11)?*

v10, 14: way back, Malachi (no, not Italian) said God would send a messenger, a 2nd Elijah, to announce his arrival. So...
• *What's Jesus saying here about John and about himself?*

v11: John's been the greatest up to this time: he understood who Jesus is. But any humble Christian since is greater: we understand more - living after Jesus' death and resurrection.

But the people of Israel weren't willing to accept John (v14) or Jesus. The response Jesus got from the religous leaders was a sulky refusal to participate (v17), and grumpy, self-centred criticism about both John and Jesus (v18).
Jesus, like John, was being misunderstood and rejected. But God's way of doing things would be proved right (v19).

👀 Pray that you'd respond to Jesus as he wants, and that you'd never tire of understanding who Jesus is.

For further study see the **OPTIONAL EXTRA** on page 59

RRRRRESPONSE

Matthew 11 v20-30

It's said learning is about the three R's: Reading, Writing (hmm, that's not an R) and Wretched school lunch (nor's that, more of an aaaargh...). Well, today it's five: Rejection, Repentance, Revelation, Relationship and Rest.

Last time, Jesus criticised those who'd seen John and himself first-hand - but hadn't repented. More on that theme here:

Read Matthew 11 v20-24.

ROCKET

Korazin, Bethsaida and Capernaum were all towns near the sea of Galilee. See their unrivalled privilege (v20, 21), but woeful response (v20a) and its inevitable result (v22).

Shock 1: Even Tyre & Sidon, Gentile towns noted for immorality and God-less arrogance, would get lighter punishment.

Shock 2: Sodom was a disgustingly perverted city which God bombed with sulphur. Capernaum was Jesus' home town...

• *Would this give its citizens any special treatment (v23-24)?*

• *Why was Capernaum's crime so much more serious?*

Now we've had the privilege of learning about Jesus.

• *What responsibility does that place on us?*

Read v25-30.

REASON

Matt's shown us a few individuals who've trusted Jesus, but generally all Jesus has met with is a blatant refusal to change.

• *Why does Jesus say there was such a response (v25)?*

It's been God's choice and plan all along (v26): the way of Jesus isn't within reach of proud, religious know-it-alls: it's only for those prepared to come in total dependence (v25b).

What a great invitation (v28): people then felt hugely burdened by all the religious demands placed upon them.

• *What is Jesus promising (v28b, 29b)?*

Jesus offers escape from the burden of man-made religion. And, to come, we'll enjoy God's rest: with him, forever. Great! But his 'rest' now (v29) will mean a yoke: there are demands to following Jesus. But compared to everything else, living under Jesus' rule, as he equips us, is - easily - the best.

• *As we come to Jesus, what will we find (v29)?*

Come to Jesus for the first time, perhaps; maybe you need to come back to him, with all your concerns. Accept his invite.

For further study see the **OPTIONAL EXTRA** on page 59

YEAH, AND THE REST
Matthew 12 v1-14

Rest? You jest! The Pharisees had turned the Jewish religion into anything but that. And one aspect where they'd really laid rules down thick was the Sabbath, the Jews' day of rest ('Sabbath' means rest). They'd expressly forbidden 39 areas of activity on the Sabbath - which probably made the day about as stress-free as a baby with a migraine.

Watch the big match here: Jesus 8, Pharisees 0.

 **Read Matthew 12 v1-8.**

No, no, no, no, no

The disciples' action (v1) wasn't unlawful, but the Pharisees said it was (v2).

• What's their motive (v2), do you think?

OK, the first five areas where they'd goofed up:

1. What should they have known from Old T history (v3-4)?

2. What should they have known from temple custom (v5)?

3. How had they misunderstood Jesus (v6)?

4. How had they misunderstood God's priorities (v7)?

5. How had they missed Jesus' status and authority (v8)?

v3: David: yes, even the great king David did that...

v6: the temple was the focus of God's presence with his people (so... what's Jesus saying about himself?). And **v8:** 'Son of Man', ie the long-awaited rescuer/ruler sent by God.

Read v9-14.

No, no and, again, no

v10: for the Pharisees, non-emergency healings (ie, not life-threatening situations) weren't to be done on the Sabbath.

6. What did Jesus point out about their own customs (v11)?

7. How were their values totally out of order (v12)?

8. What's Jesus' right understanding of the law (v12b)?

Incredibly, the man who couldn't stretch out his hand could do so as he trusted Jesus' authority (v13).

Explain the humiliated Pharisees' sinister reaction (v14).

This passage isn't about Sundays or rules. It's about Jesus. As the Messiah, he came to complete what was in the Old T. So serving God now meant following Jesus. Something those Pharisees weren't prepared to do.

• In what ways is Jesus great, according to this passage?

Take time to praise him as we should.

14

For further study see the **OPTIONAL EXTRA** on page 59

DRIVING TEST
Matthew 12 v15-37

A crowd in conversation. You lazily chuck in a comment. Uh oh. Bad reaction. You spot it, and start backing off ('OK, it was a just a careless...' etc). But they've begun offloading at you ('How dare...'). You wince.

Some of that now in Matthew, with further reactions to Jesus. There's a crowd (v15), a comment (v24) and a strong reply (v25-37). And big differences to the situation above:

1. The Pharisees fully meant what they said. No apology.
2. Jesus' measured reaction was fully justified.

 Read all of Matthew 12 v15-37 please.

Think why Matt gives another quote from the Old T (v18-21).
• *What do Jesus' actions (v15b) tell us about him (v17)?*

People wrongly expected a hard, kick-in-the-Romans type Messiah: instead, Jesus came just as the Old T said he would.
• *What marked Jesus out (from v18-21)?*
• *What had he come to do (v18b, 20b)?*

Yes! This is Matthew's big point. Jesus' mission is not limited, it's to the 'nations', it's for the world (v21): to those who would receive him - unlike most of the Pharisees and Jews then. Dramatic healing (v22): the guy had an evil spirit *and* couldn't see or speak. Sum up the Pharisees' view of it (v24).

Jesus' reply works like this:
a) How could such an inconsistent view (v24) be true?
• *See that in v25-28? What should they have realised (v28)?*

b) It's Jesus' job to defeat Satan and stop his activity (v29).
c) A persistent denial of Jesus' authority and refusal to submit to him is, frankly, unforgivable (v30-32).
• *Does this help make sense of v32b?*

d) Words reveal people's 'hearts': like produces like (v33).
• *What did the Pharisees' accusation reveal (v34-35)?*
• *Why was that ultimately serious (v36-37)?*

 Don't back off now. Jesus has said...

    ... people are either with him or against him.

        ... those who refuse to acknowledge Jesus' right

            to run their lives won't ever find forgiveness.

                ... your words (especially careless ones)

                    reveal the real you.

We urge you to take your reaction to God.

For further study see the **OPTIONAL EXTRA** on page 60

REPEAT: REPENT

Matthew 12 v38-50

Great healing. False accusation. And a fierce reply.
OK, guess what the Pharisees said to Jesus next...

👀 **Read Matthew 12 v38.**

Can you believe it? After all that, they wanted *more*?
Chs. 11-12 have shown people's reactions to Jesus so far.
Here, the Pharisees want a 'sign' as proof of Jesus' identity.
• *Why was this wrong?*

Guess what Jesus said back to them...

👀 **Read v39-40.**

• *Why are they rightly called 'adulterous' (v39)?*

This whole passage, in fact, is Jesus' criticism of that generation, represented by its religious leaders. Jesus promised them
one sign more - but they'd have to wait for it.
• *What was it (v40-42)?*

Just like in the days of the Old T prophet Jonah, it would be
outsiders - Gentiles - who'd turn to God. That would be the
sign. But Jesus said these Pharisees had enough evidence

already (v41-42).
• *How should they have responded to Jesus already? Why?*

If outsiders like the Ninevites (in Jonah's time) or the Queen
of Sheba (in Solomon's time) had listened to God's spokes-
men, how much more responsible was that generation?
• *What about ourselves?*

👀 **Read v43-45.**

Half-hearted repentance isn't enough. There's no point trying
to change a little (as in v44): Jesus must be given control.
• *Otherwise, what's the inevitable result (v45b)?*

OK, guess the response Jesus does want...

👀 **Read v46-50.**

Practical obedience: buckling down to putting his will first.
• *Then what's the great promise here (good ol' v50)?*

It's easy to criticise the Pharisees and ignore Jesus ourselves.
• *Do you pick and choose when you want to obey God?*
• *In what do you need to yield to his authority?*

THIS WAY   NO! THIS WAY

16 ❌

For further study see the **OPTIONAL EXTRA** on page 60

HEAR HERE

Matthew 13 v1-9

(Editor's note: sorry, this page was written in a hurry. If you'd prefer just to do the reading and call it quits, please do so. Today's merely a collection of trivial teasers. Apologies.)

Teaser one: Matt's been giving us a string of reactions to Jesus' authority in chs. 11-12. You know, we've said it often. We've seen enthusiastic acceptance to outright rejection. Yes, but *why* was it like that? Why didn't people turn to follow Jesus in huge numbers? Couldn't they see who he was? Any ideas?

Well, in ch. 13 Matt explains why there was a mixed response.

Read Matthew 13 v1-9.

(Ed's note: as said before, you've probably had enough by now. Don't feel bad about taking time off.)

Teaser two: Jesus is hardly going about things the right way, is he? Good start (v1) to go public, and what a great opportunity (v2)! But what does he do with it (v3)? He tells them stories, those parables... but *why*? Why not make your teaching obvious, Jesus? Why be so incredibly cryptic? Any ideas?

(Ed's note: come on, get the hint. I'm filling this page up with my comments. Why not use this Bible-reading and praying time to sort out other stuff you're worried about right now. Go on, you must have lots to do.)

Teaser three: maybe he's not being cryptic. Nice little story, isn't it? Doubtless the crowds enjoyed it: it must have been right up their street (well, in their field). But why tell 'em something they knew already? Anyone with half an agricultural brain knew this stuff. Nothing significant here, is there? Any ideas?

(Ed's note: if you haven't got stuff to keep you busy, then go and do something you enjoy. Go on, clear off, have a laugh.)

Teaser four: is v9 a joke? Everyone's got ears. And it can't be a pun (ears of corn, perhaps? No!) Doesn't everyone with ears hear? How can they *not* do so? Any ideas?

(Ed's note: still here? What for? Don't be a nerd. Grow up. And don't bother looking to see if there's an Optional Extra.)

HIDE AND SEED

Matthew 13 v10-23

OK, Jesus, explain yourself - and answer the teasers, please. (Editor's note: and we'll unravel the threads of the last study...)

👀 **Read Matthew 13 v10-17.**

• *Why didn't he explain the parable to the crowds (v11-13)?*

Surprising? We think we've got Jesus sorted and then - wham! - he's shocked us again. He's saying (isn't he?) that he spoke in parables to *hide* truth, not reveal it. So now explain v9.

God's truth has to be revealed (v11). It's not gained by natural insight. And God chooses to whom he'll reveal it. Those serious about following Jesus, those who asked him questions (like the disciples, v10) were given an explanation. Those who weren't, who didn't, were left in the dark.
• *That's what v12's about, right?*

Jesus fulfils the pattern of Isaiah (v14-15): God's saving message gets rejected due to the spiritual dullness of its hearers. See in contrast, how the disciples responded (v16).
• *What made them so infinitely privileged (v17)?*

👀 **Read v18-23.**

Four responses to the 'message of the kingdom' (the news that in Jesus, God's rule has come, as Matt's said before). All 4 hear it: how do they respond, why and with what result?
The casual (v19):

The shallow (v20-21):

The pre-occupied (v22):

The understanding (v23):

v23: only hearing and understanding (ie, accepting the truth and its demands) brings forth fruit. The mixed response to Jesus isn't the fault of his teaching. No, it's his hearers.

But there's encouragement here: there will be a harvest (v23)! Some will respond, turn to Jesus and keep going with him. Note what could put us off: trouble and persecution (v21), worry and self-sufficiency (v22), the work of the devil (v19).(Ed's note: remember getting distracted in the last study?)
• *How do you react to today's teaching?*

• *How are you encouraged? How are you warned?*

👀 Do watch your response, won't you?

For further study see the OPTIONAL EXTRA on page 60

HANG ON FOR HARVEST

Matthew 13 v24-43

Sermon writers, here's a deal. We provide the headings, you study the passage. Fair? Here are three stories:

About weed, seed and breed.

(Breed? Well, Aussies probably pronounce bread like that.)

Or about a field, a yield and some dough.

(If all your headings rhyme, people think it's a fix).

Or about sowing, growing and doughing.

(Yeah, and what sort of word is that?)

OK, if you're still not satisfied, do the following...

Read Matthew 13 v24-30.

Jesus is back with the crowds (see v36).Three parables about the growth of his rule (his 'kingdom'). Explanation next.

Read v36-43.

The weeds were darnel - a poisonous plant that looked very much like wheat. Identify what's what in the story (v37-39).

• *What's the point of the parable, then? v30, 40 should help.*

Read v31-32.

• *How did the mustard seed start out? And finish?*

• *So, get the point?*

Read v33-35.

You couldn't see it happening, but the yeast would work through masses (cor, 22 litres, unbelievable) of flour.

• *Get the point?*

Shock again, v34: Jesus concealing his truth from the crowds.

The weeds

The sower parable showed there'd be a mixed response to Jesus. This parable says people's response will only become fully clear when God judges, dividing people into two groups. For now, the growth of God's kingdom is essentially *hidden*.

• *Until when? What exactly will happen then (v41-43)?*

The seed

Unimpressive, small beginning, but a huge end result.

• *Given the parable before, when will this be seen?*

She kneads

The yeast was hidden, but its final effect was widespread.

• *What's Jesus teaching about life under his rule?*

• *Why are his disciples, Christians today, to be patient?*

WORTH MIRTH

Matthew 13 v44-52

Three more parables about the kingdom of heaven. Pile in!

Read Matthew 13 v44.

GEDDIT?

An unexpected discovery of hidden treasure.
• *How excited was the guy? How did he show it?*
• *What's the point of the parable?*

Read v45-46.

GEDDIT?

Pearls were highly prized and fetched fantastic prices.
• *How was this guy different from the one in v44?*
• *How was he similar?*

Two parables, one point: see the final phrase in each? So it's worth everything to live under Jesus' rule, in a relationship with him: these two extravagantly sold everything for it. The first (v44) stumbled across Jesus, the other (v45-46) searched for him, but both realised the infinite value of what they'd found.

Read v47-50.

GEDDIT?

• *How is this similar to the parable of the weeds (v24-30)?*

See how Jesus explains the point of it in v49, right?
Only at the end will God's work of dividing people be done.

Read v51-52.

GOT IT!

Of course, understanding... recall v13, 14, 15, 19, 23?
• *How was the disciples' understanding made possible?*
• *What was the result (v52)?*

Maybe it's a dig at the religious leaders: only the disciples can pass on new and brilliant treasures (not just Old T law) - because they've been given understanding of Jesus.
They've received 'treasure' - and are to pass it on to others.

GOT THAT?

v49-50 remind us how eternally valuable knowing Jesus is. Note down the things you value about your relationship with Jesus.

• *Are you celebrating what you've found, as the guy in v44?*

Perhaps you'd like to tell Jesus what you wrote down.

For further study see the **OPTIONAL EXTRA** on page 61

HEADING OFF
Matthew 13 v53 - 14 v12

Almost all those parables divided people: into those who were for Jesus and lived under his rule - and those who refused to.

Next, Matt gives more reactions to Jesus' authority which show that divide even more. Some people were increasingly hostile, but a handful demonstrated faith (just wait for the great highpoint of ch. 16...). So, here's a rapid double response:

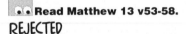**Read Matthew 13 v53-58.**
REJECTED

• *Does 'rejected' sum up what happened, do you think?*

Jesus' home town (v54) was Nazareth.
• *What's the locals' problem (v54b & 56b)?*
• *What can't they reconcile that with (v55)?*

Sceptical, disbelieving, belittling, patronising, hateful people.
• *Any other descriptions come to mind? From which verses?*
• *How could they react in such a way (v57a, 58)?*

Jesus is in no mood to change it (v57). That's their lookout.

Read ch. 14 v1-2.
DEJECTED

v1: 'tetrarch', ie Herod was the official, local ruler in Galilee.
• *Who did he think Jesus was?*
• *Does 'dejected' amply describe Herod's reaction?*

Before you finish your reply on that, v3-12 will explain why Herod was panicking (v2). Here's the background to it:

Read v3-12.
EJECTED

(Sure, 'ejected' rhymes, but you can't really talk about someone getting their head ejected can you? No, not funny at all.)
• *So why was Herod fearful of Jesus?*

It was the pits: Herod had divorced his wife (illegal in Jewish law), remarried his half-brother's wife (illegal), had a drunken, probably all-male birthday party, made a rash promise to his step-daughter, and got tricked by his new wife into beheading (illegal) John without a trial (illegal). Revolting.

Two clear-cut reactions to Jesus' authority: offence and fear. More to come next.

Thank Jesus for enduring such response.

BREAD ROLE

Matthew 14 v13-36

Authority and response: two more events now on that theme. Both might be familiar stories to you, but we're going to throw down the gauntlet (if only we could find one) and suggest the *meaning* might not be. Outraged? Well, read the lot, then work out which of the ten statements below are true or false.

Read Matthew 14 v13-36.

Bread (v13-21)

1. Jesus wanted to avoid the crowds (v13-14).
2. The disciples' reaction (v15) was understandable.
3. The miracle (v19) showed Jesus' supernatural power.
4. The crowds suddenly got their packed lunch out (v20).
5. The disciples should have provided food themselves (v16).

Water (v22-36)

6. Jesus had had enough and needed space (v22).
7. The disciples' reaction (v25) was understandable.
8. Peter is an example to us of a hero of faith (v28).
9. Jesus thought so too (v31).
10. The disciples' response was right (v33).

OK, let's find some clues for the answers:

Qn 1 (&6): Jesus snuck off (v13, 22, 23) not because he was fed up with the crowds (see v14), but to pray by himself.

• *What was it exactly that made him want to pray (v13a)?*

Given that, note his surprising welcome to the crowds (v14).

Qn 2: an understandable reaction (v15)? Yes (it was remote, late and there were lots of hungry people). But No.

• *Did Jesus think it was an understandable reaction (v16)?*

• *What attitude should they have had towards Jesus?*

After all, Jesus had transformed impossible situations before...

Qn 3: true, but there's more.

• *Who alone in the world can create?*

• *So what's this miracle revealing about Jesus?*

Qn 4: rubbish. Totally.

Qn 5: no - Jesus was testing how much they'd look to him.

Qn 6: see answer to qn 1.

Qn 7: well, was it? OK, they're tired ,etc, but they've just seen a miracle in which Jesus did something only God could do.

Qn 8: better see the answer to qn 9.

Qn 9: no, but Peter's a lesson to us. Trust in Jesus is to be single-minded, whole-hearted, not questioning Jesus' power.

Qn 10: yes, but not the whole story. It's another two chapters before they realize just who it is who stands among them.

The miracles showed Jesus exercising the power of God. And he wanted his disciples to bring every impossible situation to him - and to trust him, his compassion and power.

• *Why are we so slow to learn this?*

For further study see the **OPTIONAL EXTRA** on page 62

COME CLEAN

Matthew 15 v1-20

Cleanliness is next to godliness

• Is this proverb found in the Bible? If so, where?

Why do we ask? Well, the Pharisees, who thought they were the true leaders of God's people, had a question for Jesus - about one of their own sayings. You might just recognise it:

Read Matthew 15 v1-2.

Is...

The Pharisees, arriving from the big city, were wound up (v2). How dare Jesus' disciples break one of their wise sayings?

Read v3-9.

...cleanliness...

Jesus went on the attack (v3).

• What did his example show about the Pharisees' religion?

Think what was the most important thing for them (v3)..

• What was the horrible result (v6b)?

• How did Jesus sum them up? Explain...

• What had their religion done nothing to solve (v8-9)?

Read v10-11.

...next...

Jesus brought the crowd in to get the full story (v10a).

• Can cleanliness make you fit for God? Why not?

Read v12-14.

...to...

Jesus rejected the Pharisees as leaders of God's people.

• Why was he so severe on them?

Get his picture (v14)? It's like the blind trying to lead the blind: the result for them and their hearers is spiritual disaster.

Read v15-20.

...godliness?

• The parable was in v11. What was its point (v19)?

• Got a right view of yourself now? Sure?

• So what needs to happen if a person is to be fit for God?

No amount of religion can change our basic character. But Jesus came to deal with our fundamental need: our evil hearts.

Thank him that his death on the cross dealt with the problem. Ask for his help to go on changing - in character and action.

For further study see the OPTIONAL EXTRA on page 62

23

BREAD? CRUMBS...

Matthew 15 v21-39

More responses to Jesus' authority, seen in two miracles now: a healing of a demon-possessed girl and the feeding of 4,000 people from a handful of food.

Hang on! What's new? Healing, a food miracle: a case of 'been there, seen that, got the 'I was 1 of the 5,000' T-shirt'? Why are we told what seems to be fairly similar stuff? Eh?

Read Matthew 15 v21-39.

Note down all the differences you can between these events and stuff Matt's told us about already. OK? Use this table:

Verse:	Difference from previous stuff:

Found lots, or not a lot? Let's investigate.

DEMON AND DOGS (V21-28)

T & S (v21) were mentioned in ch. 11: proud, immoral places.

• *What's the most important bit of info about them?*
The woman (v22) is Canaanite, ie a pagan local. So what?

Cracked it? It's fantastic. T & S are in Gentile (non-Jew) territory, and the woman is a Gentile, not of the people of Israel.
• *Big deal?*
Yes! Jesus came (as v24 says) to Israel, the people God had chosen to care for over all those centuries. But the woman twigged that Jesus' mission would reach far wider (v27): all types of people could come to God through Jesus. Superb! Most of you, we suspect, are Gentiles who've come to Jesus. Stop to thank God for the people who told you about him.

v28: see how Jesus' viewed her faith. She trusted him (v27)!

HEALS AND MEALS (V29-39)

• *Again, see the major difference with the 5,000 miracle?*
See who's in the crowd by their response (v31b).

Bingo! They're a bunch of Gentiles, now praising the God of Israel who'd taken care of their needs, too.
• *Had the disciples learnt from the feeding of the 5,000?*

We'll see next just why they were so slow to understand.

Today's passage marks a great development: after rejecting Israel's leaders (v1-20) when they rejected him, Jesus shows that his mission will embrace outsiders, too. Fantastic.
• *What part are you playing in passing that message on?*

For further study see the **OPTIONAL EXTRA** on page 62

SIGN LANGUAGE

Matthew 16 v1-12

YJWBI: often said at something shocking, fantastic or dopey: 'You just wouldn't believe it.' Well, it's that time now as Matt's focus shifts from the Gentiles back to the response to Jesus of the religious teachers and the disciples. Let's talk it through.

Read Matthew ch. 16 v1.

What? Haven't these guys seen enough already? YJWBI, eh?
• *Was the request sincere (v1)? What were their motives?*

Think of the result if Jesus said 'Yes' or 'No' to their request.

Read v2-4.

YJWB etc, no. 2.
• *Why was his reply clever? How was he condemning them?*
• *What did he say they were able/not able to do?*

The 'signs of the times' were that, in Jesus, God had arrived...

Read v5.

Top humour. The bunch of 12 had just witnessed two major food miracles, with platefuls left over.. and what did they do? Left the packed lunch in the fridge! YJW etc, no. 3!

Read v6-7.

Jesus warns them, but they miss the point totally. YJ no. 4...

• *What was Jesus teaching them (v6)?*
• *What were they more worried about (v7)?*

Read v8-12.

YJ etc for the last time. Jesus had to tackle their immediate worry ('er, we forgot the food, Jesus') before explaining more.
• *Why needn't they have worried about food (v8-10)?*
• *What should they have been concerned about (v11b-12)?*

Yeast works through a whole batch of dough, right? So wrong teaching, from religious leaders who refused to recognise Jesus' identity, was getting everywhere.
See how Jesus sadly had to describe the disciples (v8a).
Recall two ways their response here to Jesus was inadequate.

Remember the contrast with the Gentile woman (15 v27-28).
Next time, Jesus spells out what true faith involves.
Ask God to help you trust him - in the way *he* wants you to.

IN THE PICTURE

Matthew 16 v13-20

Don't you just hate jigsaws? Like *really* hate? You hate the Christmas guest who suggests doing one, you hate the thousands of pieces, you hate the way they all look alike, you hate the frustration of not finishing. It's a nightmare.

Ever since ch. 1, Matt's been building up a picture for us of who Jesus is. But the disciples can't put the picture together. Then, suddenly, Peter slots in the final piece. At last...

Read Matthew 16 v13-14.
Working it out

v13: 'Son of Man' was a title Jesus often used for himself.
* *What was the current public opinion about Jesus (v14)?*

Those people (v14) were all prophets who spoke God's word.
* *Was that a right description of Jesus, too?*

Read v15-20.
Slotting it in

The question became directly personal, didn't it (v15)?
* *What incredible truth did Peter realise (v16)?*
* *How is Jesus different from John the Bap, Elijah and Jerry?*

Peter twigged that this guy was both God and human in one person. God's chosen Messiah was in town: the rescuer and ruler God had promised repeatedly since practically the start of the world. This is the one the Old T had been waiting for!

* *What else did Peter say about him, and God (v16)?*
* *Could he take any credit for his understanding (v17)?*

Jesus told Peter his role in the building of God's true people - those who belong to Jesus (v18). Peter would hold the 'keys of the kingdom': he'd have teaching authority within the church.
* *That's a body of people that will last for... how long (v18b)?*

The jigsaw's complete! Well, the main character was clear. But some of the detail needs to be looked at again:
* *Why on earth were they not to tell anyone (v20)?*

Remember what sort of a ruler/rescuer the Jews expected? Now think what would happen if word got out that Jesus was going to wade in and dust up the Romans...
No, the disciples had to learn what sort of Messiah Jesus was before they could start talking about him. That's next.

Tell Jesus your own reply to v15. Don't just repeat the right answer, tell him everything. Ask him to help you understand.

For further study see the **OPTIONAL EXTRA** on page 63

DEATH ROW?

Matthew 16 v21-28

It was going so well: all those responses to Jesus and then... Peter clinched it: Jesus - that's God stepping into his world. Then it all went horribly wrong. Peter had completed the picture, but failed to observe the vital background detail.

Read Matthew 16 v21-23.
Getting it wrong

v21: they'd grasped who he was, so Jesus could explain more.
• *What had he come to do (v21)? Why the 'must' about it?*

Think why Peter was outraged (v22) and Jesus at him (v23).
• *Whom did Jesus see behind Peter's rebuke?*
• *Why was it a stumbling-block for Jesus?*

Think back: the devil earlier tempted Jesus to turn aside from his rescue mission, to avoid the cross. Jesus again says: 'No. There's no other way set for me.' Hence the lecture to Peter. Contrast v23 with v17 (spot the bonehead).

Read v24-28.
Getting it right

We've learnt Jesus' purpose (v21). Now he tells us what's expected of his disciples. They must follow that *same* route.

If you saw someone carrying a cross in those days, you knew where they were heading, right? 'Denying oneself' meant just that: giving up the right to live. (Now read that once more.)

• *So what must characterize the disciple of Jesus (v24)?*

That's the point, too, of v25-26. See the way to find life? It's worth losing everything to gain it, isn't it (v26)?
• *Why is it vital to make the right choice about Jesus (v27)?*

Getting at you

Most of us would like an unembarrassing Jesus who cuddles sheep, says we're OK and doesn't ask too much. Instead, we find a Jesus who unsettles and disturbs us.

There's no other way to follow. Jesus went to the cross. We know his way is the route to life, true life. But we cling on to hoping Jesus won't mind if we don't take him that seriously.
• *How can we?*

Maybe it's time to ask his forgiveness, to ask him to help you realise who Jesus really is, and to get going again making Jesus everything you live for. Please do so.

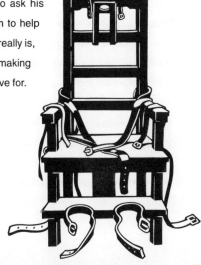

CLOUD 'N' CROWD

Matthew 17

Ch. 16 was a roller-coaster for the disciples: a real highpoint when they realised who Jesus is. A stomach-churning downer when they learnt what he'd come to do. Then that life-threatening twist of what it would mean to follow him.

Exhausted? Well, Jesus now encourages three of them with a glimpse behind the scenes: a vision of Jesus and a direct word from God. Another up-and-down chapter. Seat belt on?

Read Matthew 17 v1-12.

Highs

Jesus was 'transfigured': his whole appearance changed (v2). Ever looked at the sun or pure light? Here's Jesus: he's eye-dazzlingly pure, glorious, the unique source of light.

• *Who were Moses and Elijah?*

Right! They represent the Old T law and prophets.

• *What did Peter think he was doing (v4)?*

Brain in gear! This moment couldn't last. Why not? See v12? Then v5, a cloud: representing the awesome presence of God.

• *Which of the three characters did God speak about? Why?*

• *What were the four things he said about him (v5)?*

Here's God's confirmation that the disciples' understanding of Jesus as his chosen Messiah was right. Great assurance!

• *But why were they not to tell anyone (v9)?*

Same as 16 v20: people would hail Jesus as a Roman basher.

• *How would Jesus be treated like John the Bap (v12)?*

Read v14-23.

Lows

They returned to a scene of conflict.

• *What was Jesus' view of the disciples (v17, 20a)?*

The disciples should have trusted Jesus' authority. Even little faith (v20) can move obstacles that seem immovable.

• *What did Jesus need to remind them about (v22-23)? Why?*

Read v24-27.

And in-betweens

Jesus' priorities: he'd pay the temple tax, although it was God's place. He wasn't going to cause trouble on a side issue.

• *Will you keep a right view of Jesus?*

God's Son: the unapproachable glorious ruler for ever, who opted to leave heaven, enter our world and experience death.

• *As he was raised to life again, what will you say to him now?*

• *How much do you take in what he says?*

• *Will you rely on him to help you live as he demands?*

For further study see the OPTIONAL EXTRA on page 64

NO KIDDING

Matthew 18v1-14

(Why is this page so dull, guys? Where are the square eyes? Where's the graphics guy gone? Holiday? What about bold and italic bits? It's unimpressive, looks really insignificant.) Good! You're getting the idea. Better keep going...

Read Matthew 18 v1-5.

Jesus talked last time about tax, about big guys in authority hoiking money from little people. That nudges the disciples: right, so who are the big guys of those who know Jesus (v1)?
• How did Jesus' reply completely overturn such thinking?

Children were unimportant in that society: to be looked after, certainly not looked up to. Mere 'not-yet-adults.'
Jesus' action (v2) was shocking, his teaching (v3-5) more so: disciples should be 'like children': ie, having the same status, being insignificant, unimpressive, willing to be nobodies. So...
• What action is required from Jesus' disciples (v3a, 4a)?

Such a change isn't just for those who are already disciples: it's the only way to come to know Jesus (v3b). Clear?

v5: 'a child like this' refers to v3-4. It's a Christian who's chosen a position of unimportance. (Now didn't Jesus do that?)
• So what is greatness, according to Jesus?

Read v6-9.

v6: 'little ones' (also in v10, 14) means ordinary Christians.

• What must every Christian be careful of (v6)?

Get the picture (v6b)? Such action is so dreadful that a quick drowning would be a merciful judgment.
• Why must every Christian also watch themselves (v8-9)?

Get the picture? Ruthlessly cut out what causes you to sin. OK, so what does? Note it here, and the action you'll take.

Read v10-14.

• What should be our attitude to weaker Christians (v10)?
• Why? What's God's attitude to those who go astray (v14)?

Then that is what we should imitate.
• Which younger/newer/weaker Christians must you help?
• How and when will you do this?

More next on how Christians are to relate to one another.

FORGIVE AND REGRET?

Matthew 18 v15-35

Would you forgive a Christian friend if they...

a) wore embarrassing, open-toed sandals in your company?

b) borrowed and broke your CD player?

c) upset your closest friend with an unhelpful comment?

d) humiliated you publicly?

e) apologised for each of these?

How big is your forgiveness? Jesus talked last time about care for 'little ones', the ordinary Christians. Now he says what to do when they goof up and commit sin. Two clear orders:

Read Matthew 18 v15-20.
POINT IT OUT

Tread carefully: don't rush up to others to retaliate, but out of concern for his walk with God. Jesus has said already in Matt we must watch ourselves before pointing the finger at others.

• How should the wrong be pointed out first of all (v15)?

• How should the wrongdoer respond (v15b)?

Only then should others be brought in: to to help him listen (v16a, 17). If he refuses, he should be left alone (v17).

• How do you listen to others' careful criticism?

Read v21-35.
LET IT GO

v21: Peter thought he was being unduly generous, too.

• Is Jesus' answer to be taken literally? So what's he saying? As this parable will now illustrate...

v24: a 'talent' was the highest unit of currency, and 10,000 the highest Greek number. Geddit? It's like saying 'a billion'.

v28: a few hundred 'denarii': ie, just a few quid, in contrast.

Isn't the guy bananas? Isn't he a screw loose? How could he accept forgiveness for a debt he could never repay and then beat up a servant who owed him a handful of gobstoppers?

Jesus says that's just the sort of thing that could happen among Christians. But it mustn't.

• How should the guy in the story have behaved (v33)?

• What point does Jesus make from it (v35)?

If we've turned to Jesus, we're forgiven by him. Forever. And we must be eternally grateful.

• Then what's our responsibility? That v35 again...

• What attitudes to others do you need to change?

For further study see the OPTIONAL EXTRA on page 64

THE Y FILE

JOB: The Introduction

The young child gets mercilessly picked on. He cries all the way home from his first day at school and sobs into his pillow. Why is life like this?

The old man's speech is slurred. A stroke has snatched his ability to speak. He thinks: 'Wouldn't it have been better if…?' Why is it like this?

Cancer strikes a young mum. A happy personality is turned into a devastated dependent. The fear is crippling too. Why?

The business executive is in line for promotion. Then a car crash with a drunk driver maims him. He'll never recover. Or get his job back. Never feel that justice has been done. Why?

The teenager never felt more lonely in a crowd. She'd never go to a party again. Not now she was in a wheelchair. Why is it like this?

Why do bad things happen to good people And why do Christians sometimes seem to take a double dose? Doesn't God care? Or is he powerless to do anything about it?

You'd expect us now to say: 'Come to the book of Job to find the answers, guys,' in that sassy, perky kind of way you're used to in *The Ichthus File.* If so, we're going to disappoint.

The book of Job doesn't provide the quick 'put your money in, get your bubble gum out' sort of answers to the problem of suffering. But it does lead us to God. And it's only in the awesome presence of God that we can begin to get a right view on life's very real hardships. Answers we many not find here, but it will change our *attitude*.

These studies are searching ones. Job won't just stretch our minds, but test our character. It demands we face unexplained suffering – and be ready for more to come. We trust it will push you into a more real relationship with God.

Many of the following studies may feel like they're left hanging, unresolved. That's simply because we need to get a grasp of the book as a whole before learning its lessons. We'll do that thoroughly in the final study.

WHY ME?

NOW
Job 1 v1-12

Each study in Job has commentary from our resident expert Anna (surname: Lysis). Anna (no, it can't be spelt Ana) will interrupt every so often. Like now, for example.

Anna: Hi! This may help: chs. 1-2 say what happened to a bloke called Job. Chs. 3-37 give Job's and others' reactions to that. Chs. 38-42 give God's reaction to those discussions.

**Read Job 1 v1-5.**
On earth

• *In what ways was Job great? Describe...*
His situation (v2-3):
His character (v1):
His habits (v4-5):

Anna: some guy! So keen to live right for God that he made sure every possible sin of his children - even what they might have thought - was forgiven (v5a). It was his 'regular custom.'
• *What does that show about his relationship with God?*

**Read v6-12.**
In heaven

Anna: whoa, incredible. We get a glimpse of the action in heaven. We're taken behind the scenes. Job never gets this view at all. That's worth remembering.

v8: God brings Job to the attention of Satan, 'the accuser'.
• *How highly does God commend Job (v8)?*
• *How does Satan challenge that (v9)?*

Summarise...
God's view: Job is...
Satan's accusation: Job is...   only because...

• *What does this accusation make God out to be?*

Anna: v9 is a key to the book: is Job only godly 'cos God's given him lots of good things? See what's at stake? God's honour. Satan's suggesting: 'People only trust you God when you bless them. It's like you have to buy people's allegiance.'

• *But how confident is God in Job (v12)?*
• *Who remains in ultimate, universal control (v12b)?*

 Hang on to discover what happened next. For now, think how you'd respond to a series of personal disasters.
• *What would it do to your relationship with God?*

For further study see the **OPTIONAL EXTRA** on page 65

POW

Job 1 v13- 2 v10

The accuser said Job was 'a bought man': only following God because he got such a good deal out of it. Really?

Read Job 1 v13-22.
Strike one

• *What did Job lose?*
• *What caused each disaster (v15, 16, 17, 19)?*
• *Which loss was the worst?*

See the frighteningly intense speed of it all (v16a, 17a, 18a).
• *How did Job respond in action and words (v20-21)?*
• *What does he say is the cause of the disasters?*

Note down your immediate reaction to Job's behaviour.

Anna: Dunno about you, but I don't react like Job. What about some anger at God, Job? Why not wallow in self-pity and cry 'Why me'? Instead, the first thing he does is drop to his knees to recognise God *is* God. Although he cannot understand what's happened, he submits. And even praises God (v21b).

• *How does v21-22 answer Satan's accusation?*

Read ch. 2 v1-10.
Strike two

More debate in heaven, another challenge by Satan (v4), who refuses to admit defeat in Job's first test.
• *Now what was to happen to Job (v5)?*
You can almost feel his pain (v7): Job sits 'among the ashes' (the local rubbish-dump), banished from being near people.
• *What else does he lose (v9)?*

See what his wife says: 'There's no point going on, Job. Why not just tell God what you really think? That'll bring an end.'
• *What does his reply (v10) show?*

His wife's view was the common view then: that if you were rich and well, it was reward from God. If you suffered, it was because you were sinful, and so deserved it. Wrong, right?

Anna: Job can't understand why these disasters had happened, but he refuses to accept a view that turns God into nothing more than Santa Claus. Isn't God bigger than that?
• *Again, what's the verdict on Job's behaviour (v10b)?*

Job recognised God's right to do as he wished, but coping with the pain and questions was awful... more next.
• *Think: how do you react to even minor illness?*
• *Can you accept good from God as well as trouble?*

For further study see the **OPTIONAL EXTRA** on page 65

In chs. 1-2, we've had a view that Job never saw: a glimpse behind the scenes in heaven, where a challenge was thrown down (1 v9): 'does Job fear God for nothing?'

See some fierce reactions now to Job's suffering:

Read Job 2 v11-13.

In quietness

Anna: no jokes, please, about Bildad the Shuhite being the smallest man in the Bible. Stick with the story.

• *What action do the three friends take?*

• *What's good about that?*

Anna: This may not seem much, but this week-long silence was the best support these guys gave Job. Everything they said (chs. 4-31) undid that good work. As we'll see.

Read ch. 3 v1-4, 11-13, 20-26.

Inquiry

Describe all the emotions Job was feeling.

• *What questions was he asking about his suffering?*

Anna: Let's face it, Job was far from satisfied, but he still refused to turn his back on God. Instead, in brutal honesty, he took all his difficult, bitter and indignant questions to God.

• *Does that characterise your relationship with God?*

Read ch. 4 v7-8, v17-19, ch. 5 v17.

Iniquity

(Hmm, we think 'iniquity' means wrongdoing. Read on!)

Eliphaz claimed (4 v12-16) his advice came from a vision.

• *What did he say was the cause of Job's suffering (4 v7-8)?*

• *Was he right?*

Anna: this pretty much sums up all that Job's friends say to him in chs. 4-31: 'you're suffering because God is angry at your sin, Job. So repent.' That's badly misplaced advice.

Read ch. 6 v8-10, 7 v20-21.

Innocence

Chs. 1-2 made it clear Job was not being punished by God for any sin he'd done. Job, rightly, protested his innocence. Often he broke off in the middle of talking to his friends to pray to God (eg, 7 v7).

• *If Job's suffering wasn't punishment from God, then what answers are there as to why he suffered so much?*

For further study see the **OPTIONAL EXTRA** on page 65

ROW
Job 8 onwards

You'll have twigged by now that most of the book of Job is a conversation. Chs. 4-31 has three 'rounds' of speeches in which Job's friends each speak to him and he replies.

We've heard Eliphaz's views. What about Bildad and Zophar? Is their first-round advice encouraging? Will it be true?

Read Job 8 v1-2, 8-13.
Bildad builds up?

• How sympathetic was Bildad?

• What did he appeal to Job to learn from (v8-10)?

Use v13 to summarise what he's saying to Job.

See what Job replied about God in 9 v21-22, v33-35. Use these verses (and 10 v1, why not) to describe Job's thoughts.

Read ch. 11 v1-2, 5-6.
Zophar so good?

• What did Zophar wish would happen (v5)?

• What did he expect that would prove (v6)?

Anna: Was this advice right? What about Bildad's? Any of it?

Job replied to Zophar in 12 v4-5.

• What did he still maintain (v4b)?

Anna: Job was in physical pain and mental turmoil. The three friends only made it worse, with their cold, arrogant judgments on what God must think of Job. See Job's view in 16 v2.

Rounds two and three of the conversation add nothing new: we simply find tempers get raised, arguments repeated.

• But what do these verses tell us more about Job?

13 v15:

19 v25-27:

23 v2-5:

God seemed inaccessible. Job was desperate, not to get his goods back or get his body healed, but for his relationship with God to be restored. He knew it was only in a relationship with God that wisdom, a right attitude, could be found.

Anna: Job's friends didn't help his real need. He wanted comfort, hope, even vindication. What he got was sharp criticism from people who thought they knew God's answers.

They talked *about* God (so they thought). Job talked *to* God.

• Which is your priority in baffling circumstances?

• *Where have all the conversations in Job got us so far?*
a) nowhere b) headache street c) confusion d) desperation
Probably all of those. Now think:
• *Where have all the conversations got Job?*

Nowhere, certainly. Worse off, yup. Confused? Well, he still maintains that God can't be punishing him for some sin of his. But he's not clearer on why such disasters have come his way and he wants answers from God. And desperate? Sure, to re-discover his intimate relationship with God.

If you feel we've got nowhere so far, you're right! After chs. 4-31, Job & co. are at stalemate. See ch. 32 v1... and groan...

But it's in ch. 32 another character appears, called Elihu. He's obviously been listening in on the conversation. And he's livid, believing the conversation has been offensive to God.

Read Job 32 v1-5.

Mr Angry

• *What three things was he angry about (v2, 3, 5)?*

Elihu was so angry he offloaded for six full chapters.
• *What does 32 v20-21 and 36 v4 tell us about his attitude?*

So when Elihu claimed to be timid (32 v6), we reply: 'Oh yeah?' Let's see what this know-it-all offered Job for advice:

a) 'Learn from and in your suffering': see ch. 33 v29-30.

b) 'God is both just and merciful': see ch. 36 v15-16.

c) 'Don't turn to evil to relieve your suffering': see ch. 36 v21.

d) 'God doesn't answer your prayer because your motives are mixed and there's sin in your heart': see 35 v9-16.

e) 'Your own view of God is wrong': see 34 v5-9.

• *Are these statements good, bad or ugly?*

Anna: hmm, intriguing. Elihu wanted Job to realise the greatness of God. Some of his advice was right. But in the end, he sided with the view of the three friends: 'You're getting what you deserve, Job.' And so he was exceedingly unhelpful.

• *Think: what things can suffering teach us?*

(PS: can someone tell us what 'yow' means please?)

For further study see the **OPTIONAL EXTRA** on page 66

WOW
Job 38-41

As Elihu raged, we're told that a storm had been brewing...

Ever been out in a thunderstorm? Awesome, eh? Stinging rain, the flash of forked lightning and explosive thunderclaps. Incredible. Until it gets too close for comfort, that is, and then it's absolutely terrifying. That intense fear of being seriously vulnerable. That feeling of having nowhere to hide.

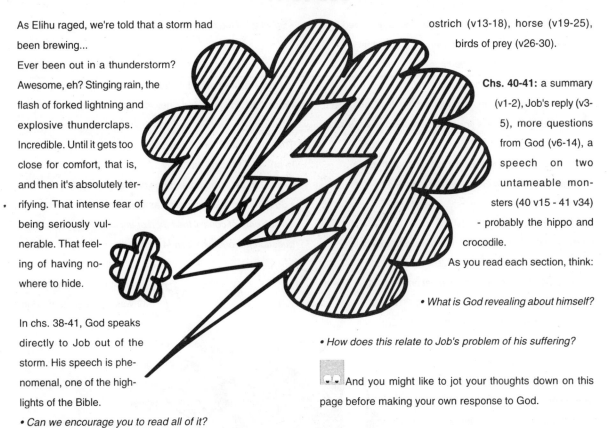

In chs. 38-41, God speaks directly to Job out of the storm. His speech is phenomenal, one of the highlights of the Bible.

• *Can we encourage you to read all of it?*

Go at your own pace. Maybe spread it out over a day or so.

Knowing this structure may help:

Ch. 38: intro (v1-3), then questions about the earth (v4-18), the elements (v19-30), and the world in general (v31-41).

Ch. 39: questions about unusual creatures on God's earth: the mountain goat (v1-4), wild donkey (v5-8), wild ox (v9-12), ostrich (v13-18), horse (v19-25), birds of prey (v26-30).

Chs. 40-41: a summary (v1-2), Job's reply (v3-5), more questions from God (v6-14), a speech on two untameable monsters (40 v15 - 41 v34) - probably the hippo and crocodile.

As you read each section, think:

• *What is God revealing about himself?*

• *How does this relate to Job's problem of his suffering?*

And you might like to jot your thoughts down on this page before making your own response to God.

No Optional Extra today: take your time on the reading.

HOW?
Job 38-41

The devil's accusation (1 v9) was that Job only served God because he paid well, right? See what's behind that?

• Is God worth serving for who he is?

Or just for what you can get out of him?

ie, it's not just suffering that's under debate. It's God himself.

• How would you express your answers using chs. 38-41?

Perhaps we could review God's speech together...

• Intriguingly, what did God give Job (38 v3)?

• Why, do you think?

God's answer was a storm of questions. For example:

In ch. 38:

• Was Job a partner with God in creation (38 v4-11)?

• Can Job call forth the sunrise (v12-15)?

• Does Job know about hidden things (v16-20)?

• Can Job control the weather (v22-38)?

See God's teasing irony in v21...

In ch. 39:

• Does Job know everything in intimate detail (v1-4)?

• Can he control a wild ox (v9-12)?

• Do birds migrate at Job's command (v26-30)?

Anna: the underlying question for Job behind all of these is: 'Just who is God?' ie, get a right attitude!

• Could you answer that, please?

• So why is God to be honoured?

Job was silenced (40 v3-5). As he looked away from himself to God, he saw himself in his true light: insignificant (v4). He couldn't take on God - how dare he ask for answers?

Then more questions follow, eg:

In ch. 40-41: catch the irony...

• Has Job the strength and power of God (40 v9)?

• So can he dispense justice as God does (40 v10-11)?

• If Job cannot control the hippo or the crocodile, how can he question the one who can (41 v9-11)?

Anna: the theme in chs. 38-39 was God's great wisdom and his detailed care. In 40 v8-14, it's God's justice that's brought to Job's attention. Then chs. 40-41 show God's limitless power.

• How have chs. 38-41 changed your view of God?

Please stop to honour God. And think how God's speech should change Job's attitude to his suffering.

For further study see the **OPTIONAL EXTRA** on page 66

BOW
Job 42

God didn't respond to Job's questions about his suffering. Instead, he showed Job his great wisdom, justice and power.

• *What new attitude would this give Job on his suffering?*

Job was told:

God has infinite wisdom: so Job couldn't conclude that God didn't know what he was doing through Job's suffering.

God is completely just: he couldn't say that God was inflicting punishment on him just for the sake of it.

God is all-powerful: he couldn't say God lacked the ability to carry out his will.

Let's hear Job's own reply:

Read Job 42 v1-6.
Reply

• *What has Job realised about:*
... God?
... himself?
... his suffering?

In chs. 1-2, we saw that sin was not the cause of Job's suffering. Throughout the story, Job has maintained his innocence. And he's questioned God, but never denied him.

• *So why the need to repent (v6)?*

Maybe we should say: 'How could he not?' Sure, he's not repenting of any sin (that might have caused his suffering). But he's just had a staggering personal encounter with God:

Job now realises his arrogance at expecting an answer from God - as if God was accountable to him! Job sees that he does not know God as he should. Hence his response.

Read v7-17.
Replay

See how God describes Job, four times (v7-8). Brilliant!
• *But what does he say about the three friends?*

v10: see how generous God was to Job.
• *What does Job receive (v10b, 11a, 12, 13, 16)?*

Anna: Job didn't get answers from God about his suffering. He got a new attitude. He realised that what was a puzzle for him to understand was not a puzzle for God. Job knew that not one part of God's creation was outside God's control.

Thank God for such an incredible book. Deep stuff!
• *How has the book of Job changed your attitude?*

For further study see the OPTIONAL EXTRA on page 67

VOW

Job - review

Let's learn from Job: it might help you to refer back to the studies as we look back at some of them now. Cheers.

NOW

Remember 1 v9? 'Does Job fear God for nothing?'
Does he only serve God for what he gets from him?
Is God worth our allegiance anyway? What's your answer?
• *Do you fear God for nothing?*
• *When your prayers go unanswered, when something dreadful happens, will you still love and honour God?*

POW

Remember 1 v21? 'The Lord gave, the Lord has taken away.'
• *What did the disaster-hit Job rightly acknowledge?*
• *Could you say the same? Do you?*

Perhaps think of your worst fear. Complete the line:
'I can face everything except...'
   • *Would you still trust God if that happened to you?*

OW

The friends' best help was their silent support (2 v11-13).
   • *Do you claim to have all the answers to friends' hardships?*
   • *How can you support them in a helpful, practical way?*

Job took all his puzzled, angry questions in life to God. His real desire was for his relationship with God. That's the one thing that will endure in time and eternity.
• *What depth is there to your relationship with God?*

YOW

Elihu was right in some of his advice. Like these two bits:
God disciplines his servants to help them grow.
Don't resort to evil, to sin, to relieve your suffering.
• *Is it better to be a carefree sinner or disciplined disciple?*
• *Does suffering teach you and lead you to God?*

HOW

Job heard God speak. And how his attitude changed: he couldn't understand, but he bowed to God's authority.
• *What must you, in hard times, cling onto about God?*

Job, an innocent man, suffered. Think New Testament now... Jesus, the perfect eternal Son of God, whose righteous life was far beyond Job's, suffered more than anyone. Jesus suffered a cruel human death - so that our relationship with God could be restored forever.
Those who live right for God do suffer, but the Bible says no disaster, not even death, can break that restored relationship between God and his people.
• *Does this change your attitude to God?*

• *How will it help you when times of trouble come?*

Thank God for Job. Even more, thank God for Jesus.

For further study see the **OPTIONAL EXTRA** on page 67

Sort the house out

1 Timothy: The Introduction

Your parents swan off on holiday. A week later, one of those painted-on blue sky postcards arrives. Wording as follows:

Hi! Having a fantastic time. Place is really nice. Dad's got sunburnt - already! Time's going all too fast.
Sorry, forgot to stock up on catfood before we left. Can you get some (it's beef and liver he likes)? And the Penningtons are coming round on the day we return. Can you give the lounge a hoover and sort the house out?
Love, Mum.

Yeah, cheers, folks. They enjoy getting a suntan while yours truly has to grovel under the sofa vacuuming up the cat hairs. Great... one of my all-time favourite jobs.

You're getting the flavour of the apostle Paul's first letter to Timothy, a young-ish Christian leader who's in charge of a church in (most likely) Ephesus. It's mid 1st century AD.

Paul's not writing really to tell Tim about his suntan. He's got more urgent matters in mind, which will involve some pretty tough work for Tim. Wording as follows:

Although I hope to come to you soon, I am writing you these instructions so that, if I am delayed, you will know how people ought to conduct themselves in God's household...
1 Timothy 3 v14-15.

Paul's got a job for Tim to do: to sort the house out. Or to be precise, to sort God's household out. To get the church in order. To get its members behaving and relating to each other as God wanted.

Like vacuuming out the cat-hairs, it would be a painfully testing job. Tim would have to confront people, challenge them, sometimes tell them off. He'd be opposed in his task. Paul told Tim it would be like a fight. But it had to be done because the church is God's household: it must live in line with God's truth. What was going on in Ephesus was far from that.

Paul gives commands for almost everyone in God's house: men, women, leaders, members, widows, slaves, rich, poor.

FALSE START

1 Timothy 1 v1-11

Ever spoken with someone from a cult? They quote from the Bible and seem to know it better than we do. But it's dangerous: they pick bits from the Bible, then use them wrongly. It's not a new problem. Paul had it in his day, even in a church he'd spent a long time in. He wrote to get Tim to rescue that church from dangerously false teachers. Sort the house out!

Read 1 Timothy 1 v1-7.
Using the Bible wrongly

Paul the apostle (v1) was specially appointed by God to teach about Jesus. And a top lad he was, too.
• *What's Tim told to do (v3)? Why (v4b)?*
• *Which words show how strongly Paul felt about this?*

v4: probably refers to writings that were popular between Old and New Testament times..
• *What was the effect of these on the church (v4b, 6, 7)?*

v4b: maybe people were using these family trees to try to prove their ancestry - as if that made them 'in' with God.
• *Instead, what's the only way to know God (v4b)?*

• *And what should that result in (v5)?*

Even worse, those false teachers wanted to be leaders (v7a).
• *Why was that impossible, according to Paul (v6-7)?*

Read v8-11.
Using the Bible correctly

v8: 'law' here = the Old T, or specifically, the Ten Commandments. As these guys were using the Old T wrongly, was the answer to stick to the life of Jesus and miss out the Old T? Er, no, pal. See what the Old T usefully points out (v9-10a).
• *What's the test of right teaching (v10b-11)?*

Right! The Old T shows God's perfect standards and leads us to the gospel: the truth of what God's done through Jesus.
Jot down what you'll learn here from:
Paul's warnings:
His commands to Tim:

• *Why are we often afraid to talk with people who hold different views about God and the Christian faith?*
• *What would you do if a speaker you heard said stuff you thought was a bit dodgy?*

Ask God to help you know your Bible well and live right.

MINUTE STEAK
1 Timothy 1 v12-20

Paul wrote to beef up Tim to take on the false teachers. Then (v11, last time) he hit on his favourite topic. Read on now as he did Gospel Gabble: could he talk for a minute about the gospel without hesitating, deviating or repeating himself?

Read 1 Timothy 1 v12-17.
The gospel and me

Gospel gobsmacked! Great stuff, Paul. But you did repeat the words 'Christ Jesus' and 'sinners' quite a lot.
• *Hold on! How do those two phrases just about sum up what Paul knew to be true about the gospel and himself?*

Describe Paul's life before he came to know Jesus (v13). Now think how the false teachers might have used that against him: 'He can't be a Christian: we know all about his past...'
• *Did Paul deny his past? How did he handle it (v13-14)?*
• *What things did he recognise had happened (v14)?*

v15: yo! Use it to say what it really means to be a Christian.

Paul rated himself the worst sinner ever (v15b): but he knew his past had been dealt with by Jesus at the cross.
• *But why on earth did God choose someone like Paul (v16)?*

Brilliant! If Paul could be changed by God, then anyone can. Explain how people should respond to Jesus (v16b).
v17 is Paul's yahoo: how he felt about what he'd just said.
• *Can you agree with a strong 'Amen'? Why/why not?*

Read v18-20.
The gospel and you

Back to the task: it was more like a war (v18).
• *What was Tim told to do (v19a)? And how (v19b)?*
• *Why was the task impossible without those qualities (v19)?*

v20 probably refers to church discipline which Paul put these men through. Until they repented of their errors or behaviour they were to be excluded from the church. Got that, Tim?
• *Why was it so vital that Tim stuck to his job?*

Paul wasn't put off by those who knew his past. He knew God had forgiven him. The good news in the gospel is that the past can be put behind us when we come to know Jesus. It's not our past that counts, but how we're living for God now.
• *Taken that in yourself?*

Now thank God for that. No hesitating, deviating, repetition...

For further study see the **OPTIONAL EXTRA** on page 68

PRAYER TONIC
1 Timothy 2 v1-8

Tim's task: ch. 2 is Paul's orders to sort out all the unruly, unhelpful, undisciplined and generally un-everything stuff that went on when the church, God's household, met together.
Those false teachers were apparently teaching that God's rescue was only for certain people, and suggesting that Christians refuse to co-operate with the Roman authorities.
Paul pours out two instructions, then opens up a six-pack of reasons why those orders were right. Drink it in...

👀 **Read 1 Timothy 2 v1-2.**
Make that a double

• What's the urgent instruction in v1?
• ...and in v2?

The 'pray for all' (v1) includes two categories Paul was very concerned about: rulers (v2) and Gentiles, ie non-Jews (v8).
Think why Paul wanted that church to pray for those groups.
• Who do you think is beyond God's reach? Are they really?
• Why do we need to pray for our rulers (v2b)?

Make up a prayer list of 'those in authority'. Who'd be on it?

👀 **Read v3-8.**
Open the six-pack

Praying this way is good, says Paul (v3).

List as many reasons as possible from v3-7 why Paul tells us to pray for everyone to be saved.
Not found six (or you've got more)? Get your head seen to. (Er, we mean, *please* check the six given in the Opt Extra).

• *How prominently does Jesus feature in Paul's reasons?*
• *What are we told here about him (Jesus, that is)?*

v3: 'mediator' = a link, bridge, peacemaker, that sort of idea.

v8 isn't telling us the position we ought to adopt as we pray. Hand-raising isn't better than hand-lowering (or vice versa). They all probably raised their hands - part of their culture. Paul's saying men must *pray* - rather than resort to their natural tendency to get aggressive and fight each other.

The key thing is the attitude of our hearts: why should God hear us is if we come with the unresolved attitudes of v8b?

Paul was trying to talk sense into the unruly church in Ephesus: to get them praying for rulers, and for everybody. 'Cos the mission of Jesus shows us that's a good thing to do.

👀 Agree? Then crack on with it.

For further study see the OPTIONAL EXTRA on page 68

ADDRESSING THE ADDRESS

1 Timothy 2 v9-15

Steady! This next bit often generates more heat than light. It's controversial, sure. But it's God's word. Step forward...

We've already learnt that some Christian men in the church were more likely to fight than pray. Now we'll see that some women thought their freedom 'in Christ' allowed them to behave as they liked: wear clothing that really got them noticed and to be pretty unruly in church. Paul spotted the dangers.

Read 1 Timothy 2 v9-10.

Dressing to kill

The precise clothing they wore wasn't the issue here. Whatever it was, it was extravagant. Show-offy. Look at us, guys!
• *What's Paul's concern for these women here?*
• *How should they demonstrate their freedom in Christ (v10)?*

• *How far should Christian girls/women follow fashions today?*
• *Why?*

Read v11-15.

Killing the address

These women wouldn't accept the teaching of the church's leaders and pushed themselves forward. Chaos, probably. But Paul was being radical here: let women learn too, guys!
• *What's the right attitude for these women to have (v11)?*
• *What is not the woman's role in the church setting (v12)?*
• *What reason does Paul give (v13)?*

For a woman to teach a congregation of men and women isn't on, says Paul. It would reverse the created order. (Hmm, this seems negative: what *can* Christian women do? Well, there's lots elsewhere in the New T. See the Opt Ext, where we'll also tackle that snorter v15.)

Paul didn't say women should dress like their parents. Phew... no, their inner character and good deeds are more important. He didn't say women have no contribution to make at church: he wanted men and women to stick to their God-given roles.
• *How does this fly in the face of current views in society of male/female roles in church? What about your views?*

• *How does today's teaching make you feel? Why?*
• *What might obeying it cost you?*
Jot down any questions you need to ask an older Christian.

It's hard, sure. But we trust in God's goodness: that he wants what's best for us. Ask him to help us submit to his word.

For further study see the OPTIONAL EXTRA on page 69

LEADING QUESTION

1 Timothy 3 v1-16

Circle some words, please, to express your own view.

a) Church leaders should be:

godly   guitar-playing   tall   bearded   trendy

single   married   male   female   have kids

middle-aged   wear suits   preachers   Christian

kind   be organised   know the Bible   hospitable

b) Church leaders should not be:

Aged under 30   American   Ugly   Rude

New Christians   Young Christians   Old Christians

Male   Female   All male   All female

Trendy   Out of touch   Untrained   Power-hungry

In ch. 3, Paul's still getting Tim to sort that church out. Now he's on about its leaders.

Read 1 Timothy 3 v1-7.

ELDER POWER

v1: in the New T, leaders are called overseers or elders or pastors. Different words, same job. Each church probably had teams of leaders - some working full-time.

• *Why is this sort of leadership called a 'noble task' (v1)?*

• *What must leaders be like? What must they do (v2-7)?*

• *Why must they have a good reputation outside the church?*

Think whether these verses alter your attitude to your church or youth group/CU leaders.

Read v8-16.

DEACON CLUE

v8: 'deacons' really means 'servants': ie, it's a much wider role than the way we tend to use it nowadays. It's right to apply it all who serve Jesus in some capacity in the church.
• *What 'tests' (v10) should be done before someone serves?*

v11: best understood as women deacons: ie, here's support for women workers in church.

v16: Paul quotes a summary about Jesus: that's the truth the church is based on (v15) and its leaders must teach.

Now think which words (at the start of the study) Paul would have circled for a) overseers b) deacons..
• *What are the responsibilities of church leadership (v2-12)?*

• *What are its rewards (v13)?*

Thank God for your leaders. Please pray for them.

BODY OF TRUTH?

1 Timothy 4 v1-8

Sounded like Paul was finishing his letter at the end of ch. 3 - all the stuff about 'Hope to come soon, get the kettle on, etc'. Anyway, he's still got more, vital stuff to say about Tim sorting the church out. Here are his instructions:

Read 1 Timothy 4 v1-5.

QUASH

Some people in Ephesus were teaching rubbish (v1-3). Tim was to quash (what a tasty word that is) such teaching. ie, sit on it, hard. Stamp it out. Quash it, basically.

• What had some people done (v1a)?

• In what ways are they described (v2)?

• And what was dangerously behind all this (v1b)?

See the exact content of their wrong teaching (v3).

• What modern equivalents do we have of such taboos?

• How does Paul answer this negative teaching in v4-5?

Presumably these people (v2) called themselves Christians. But they were teaching others seriously wrong views about how to live the Christian life and be godly.

Think why it's so important to quash wrong teaching.

Read v6-8.

AND GO

• What's Tim told here to do in terms of:
a) teaching others?
b) his own life?

That wasn't going to be easy for him, was it? No chance (v8).
• How is becoming godly like going to the gym for a workout?
• Why's it better to aim for godly living than a good body (v8)?

Neither's easy to get, but only one is ultimately worth it.
• How much are you trying to llive a godly life?
• How hard are you honestly working at it?

Don't miss the nice little dig Paul gives about the wrong teaching (v7): 'Pah! It's a load of old wives' tales. Bin it.' Yessir! Instead, train yourself to be godly. Ready to sweat over that?

For further study see the **OPTIONAL EXTRA** on page 69

LEADING ARTICLE
1 Timothy 4 v9-16

A bit of a newspaper today: lots of sections to read. Sorry, no cartoons (don't want to spoil you). Also no yawny political analysis column. And we recommend the order you read it in.

• *Do you have a leadership role over other Christians?*
Then read sections A and B.

• *Are you part of a Christian group rather than a leader?*
Then sections A and C are for you. Take your time!

After your sections, you can always spy out the other bits...

Read 1 Timothy 4 v9-10.
SECTION A: NEWS IN BRIEF

Top man Paul hit back at false teachers with fierce reminder. His reliable comments need widespread reporting (v9).

The eager apostle stressed the basis of the Christian life: it's not rules (as v3), but a total trust in God's rescue (v10).

And the chief lad recognised God's care for everyone - while knowing it's those who trust him who'll know that in full (v10b).

Now all read v11-16.
SECTION B: REVIEW

Pick out the ten (or is it nine?) commands Paul gives here.

• *Which particularly do you need to heed right now? Why?*

Tim was a special appointment in charge of a church (v13-14). But snaffle the principles for Christian leadership: teach the Bible right, live right, keep making progress.

• *How do you shape up in these three areas?*

Think what sort of example you are, using the list in v12. Note one way to improve in each.

v15 isn't saying: 'Be perfect'. But 'make progress'.

• *Why is that difference encouraging?*

SECTION C: SUPPLEMENT

Paul's talking to Tim as a leader. But v12 highlights five areas which every Christian must watch. Answer these:

Speech: how much do you think about what you say?

Life: what attitudes and actions characterise you?

Love: do you care about others much in practical ways?

Faith: what do you need to trust God about?

Purity: what motives lie behind what you say and do?

Make progress, says Paul. Turn your answers into prayers.

For further study see the **OPTIONAL EXTRA** on page 70

WIDOW WINDOW

1 Timothy 5 v1-16

• *Are you a widow?*

(Start again! That opening line is awful. A turn-off.)

• *Are you over 60?*

(And that's hardly better. This isn't The OAP File, you know.)

• *Do you like widows?*

(What sort of duff question is that, then? Do you?)

• *Do you like widows over 60?*

(Come on, we've warned you. Get it together.)

• *Do you like good-looking young widows keen to re-marry?*

(Well, er... steady, steady.)

• *Then let me introduce the gorgeous...*

(Whoa! That'll do, thanks.)

• *OK, then meet Zoe and Esme, two widows in Ephesus.*

(Ah, now we're getting somewhere.)

• *Zoe is 60-ish, a mature Christian, but has no relatives left.*

(Hmm, so how's she going to survive then? Intriguing.)

• *Esme is also a Christian. She's in her mid-thirties.*

(Where's all this leading, then?)

• *Should the church look after Zoe, Esme, neither or both?*

(Well, I never knew widows could be so interesting...)

• *What instructions do you think Paul gives Tim about them?*

●● **Read 1 Timothy 5 v1-15.**

v1-2 round off ch. 4: Paul's said Tim's task would involve

him in confrontation. These verses tell him how to do it.

• *How is he, then?*

• *When must Tim be especially careful? (See why?)*

Distinguish from v3-16 which verses are talking about Zoe and which about Esme. Note Paul's orders.

• *Whose job is it first off to care for widows (v4, 7-8)?*

But there were those who had no family still alive. Some could be put on the church's support list, others shouldn't be.

• *Which should (v9-10), which shouldn't (v11-15), and why?*

It seems that younger widows (Esme, etc) who were put on the list had promised not to-remarry but to be busy serving Christ (the 'first pledge', v12) by helping other women in the church. But they'd then got keen on marrying again (v11). Being totally looked after by the church, they weren't using their time to serve Jesus at all (v13).

• *What advice was Tim to give them (v14)?*

Well, there you have it.

(I can't believe I've just enjoyed reading about widows... and I'll remember that when I'm a widow/widower.)

• *Got the principle for all of us Christians?*

(Course. That's v4 & v8. I'll remember that, too. Cheers!)

For further study see the **OPTIONAL EXTRA** on page 70

ALL ABOUT WORTHING

1 Timothy 5 v17 - 6 v2

99% of you will have assumed the headline refers to that huge old people's home by the sea. You know, that town near Brighton. Wrong!

49% of you will be trying to make some link between old people in Worthing and widows in Ephesus. Wrong again!

1% will have given up trying to anticipate the next joke. Right! There is no joke. Just this: Worthing (as above) isn't a town. It's a verb. As in, let's get *worth-ing*. We must *worth* people.

It's Paul's big thing in ch. 5 and the first bit of ch. 6: certain people need to be worthed. (OK, they're *worthy* of special treatment, then). Last time it was widows (5 v3). Now it's the church leaders (5 v17) and, curiously, slave-owners (6 v1).

•• Read 1 Timothy 5 v17-25.
Elders

Remember who the elders were - ch. 3 v1-7?

Some, it seems, were greedy, commanding big fees for their preaching work. Paul here explains how to treat (v17-18), discipline (v19-21) and appoint them (v22, 24-25).

* Does v17 say they should get double pay? What, then?
* What's the principle here for those in Christian ministry?

See what precautions Tim should take in getting tough with the elders (v19) - and what he should do if he discovered some shady goings-on (v20).

* How seriously did Paul take this matter (v21)?
* What's the constant danger in leadership (v21b)? Agree?

v22: the 'laying on of hands' = appointing them to leadership.

* Why wasn't Tim to be too hasty?

He might reject people for leadership too fast (v24a) or accept others only to find out later what they were like (v24b).

•• Read ch. 6 v1-2.
Slave-owners

Slaves wanted their freedom, after all. And where their masters were Christians, wasn't it OK to ease up?

* What's Paul's response to such an attitude (v1-2)?
* What's his double concern (v1b)?

Draw out the principle here for the Christian at work (whether at school, college, job, home, paid/unpaid, full/part time).

* How do you measure up to this?
* Should we expect more lenient treatment if our boss/teacher is also a Christian?

Pray over what you've learned today for yourself and others.

MONEY-CHANGER

1 Timothy 6 v3-10

"It's better to be rich than poor. You get more to enjoy, you don't have to worry about being on the breadline, you always know there's something in the bank. It's kind of reassuring."
Agree? Disagree? Why?

"It's better to be poor than rich. All that worry over what to do with your money! It eats at you. Poverty does make you appreciate what you've got, the simple things in life."
Agree? Disagree? Why?

Now write down your own view:
"It's better to be _____ because...."

Catch one view kicking round the Ephesus church:
"It's better to be rich than poor. And there's no reason why each of us believers can't be rich. God wants to bless us - so by living godly lives we can expect him to reward us."
Agree? Disagree? Why?

In ch. 6, Paul exposes the church's problem: a shameless exploitation of wealth. It seems the greedy elders flattered wealthy church members in their teaching. In turn, those rich people weren't challenged at all and rewarded the elders.

That's not on, says Paul. First he addresses the greedy elders (v3-10), then he gives Tim personal instruction (v11-16, 20-21), then he talks about the rich church members in v17-19. Time to investigate how Tim should sort the house out...

Read 1 Timothy 6 v3-10.

As we'll see from the rest of the chapter, Paul doesn't say it's better to be rich *or* poor. Explain what he says:
"It's better to be _____ because...

Some elders taught that honouring God led to wealth (v5).
• *What's Paul's view of such teaching and teachers (v3-5)?*
• *What five things does their teaching result in (v4b-5a)?*

See what Paul says really is worth having (v6, 8).
• *Why, part i (v7)? Why, part ii (v9)? Why, part iii (v10)?*

Rich or poor, we still think a little bit more will make us happy.
• *What about you? Do you actually believe v6-10 are right?*

It could mean giving up life-long ambitions, goals, and habits. Going to do it? We suggest you tell God your answer.

For further study see the **OPTIONAL EXTRA** on page 71

TACKLING TACTICS

1 Timothy 6 v11-21

It's a quite unstoppable move to round off the letter. Paul, the midfield general, passes (instructions) to Tim, then to the rich wing of the church, then it's back to Tim, then Paul knocks in a beautiful finish and waves to the crowds. Glorious!

Last time, Paul was laying into those who were giving false teaching on money. Tim's got to remain true to God in the midst of all that. Here are Paul's orders to sort it out.

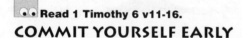**Read 1 Timothy 6 v11-16.**

COMMIT YOURSELF EARLY

v11-12: strong words, right? 'Flee, pursue, fight, take hold...' What's today's general view of the Christian life? Probably something like 'pray, don't overdo it, dialogue and be nice.'
* *What important characteristics must Tim develop?*

A powerful combination (v11): think why Tim needed each.
* *What's the 'good fight of the faith' (v12), do you think?*

v12: his 'good confession' may be his baptism - when he gave a testimony about how he wanted to serve God.
List the incentives that Paul gives Tim to persevere (v13-16).

Read v17-19.

ATTACK

Now there's orders for the rich church members.
* *What are they to be told not to do (v17)?*
* *And to do (v18)?*

Paul's not just giving a gentle hint. These are orders.
* *Why, it's not that big a deal is it? What's at stake (v19)?*

Read v20-21.

DEFEND

* *Paul's urgent summary: how must Tim be different?*

What's been 'entrusted' to him (v20)? Surely it's clear, gospel teaching on Jesus from Paul. That's what he's got to fight for. Because there'll be constant challenge to wander from it.
* *What exactly will 'guarding' the gospel involve, do you think?*

JOIN IN

For Paul, there was no easy life in following Jesus.
* *How determined are you to live as v11-12 says?*
* *How much do you stand up for Jesus - and the Bible?*

Take 1 Tim to heart. Ask God to help you make real changes.

For further study see the **OPTIONAL EXTRA** on page 71

WHAT DO I DO NEXT?

You've been jumped on by the Job, mangled by Matthew and Trampled by (1) Timothy – and you still want more?

Fear not brave fishy filer, all is not lost, for there is yet another Ichthian issue just waiting for you to get your teeth into. You can get it three ways:

1. Snip out the box top right and give it to your local Christian bookshop. They'll order it in for you every issue so that you can pop in and buy it from them. Or else stick a brick through the window and nick it. On second thoughts...

2. Carve out the middle box and get your Mum/Dad/Guardian/Zookeeper to write out a cheque, or fill in the credit card details. We'll send you the next six issues (one every two months) entirely for free. No only kidding - for £12.50 - you save £2.50 and it's delivered hot and steaming with a radiation warning on the packet straight to your door. Alternatively, you could get hold of a credit card and ring us up on 0181-947 5686 to order it. On third thoughts, ask their permission first.

3. Slice off the bottom box and hand it to your youth club leader - get him to arrange for you and others in the group to get regular copies, and you could all come away with a major cash bonus... it may do him/her a lot of good as well.

Whichever way round you do it, you'll be guaranteed a regular fishy feedup from the best book on this – or any other for that matter – planet. Go for it!

DEAR MR BOOKSHOP MANAGER

I'd like to order regular copies of *The Ichthus File* - daily Bible reading notes. Please order me up a regular copy, and I promise I'll call in and pick 'em up. I'll even pay for them!

Name .... Tel ....

Address ....

.... postcode ....

Note to Bookseller:
The Ichthus File is published by St Matthias Press, P.O.Box 665, London SW20 8RL. Call 0181-947 5686 to order, or fax through on 0181-944 7091.

DEAR ICHTHUS FILE TEAM

I'd like to order regular copies of *The Ichthus File* - deliver them straight to my door or I'll explode.

Name .... Tel ....

Address ....

....

Postcode .... Last issue received: ......

Make cheques payable to *St Matthias Press* and send to:
P.O.Box 665, London SW20 8RL.

OR PAY BY CREDIT CARD:

Card no .... Expiry date ....

Name on card ....

Billing Address (if different from above) ....

....

....

DEAR YOUTH GROUP LEADER

What do you mean you've never heard of the Ichthus File?
Call Tim or Ches on 0181-947-5686 to talk about getting the rest of your group on the best Bible notes around...

Optional eXtra

You've finished the study, but want to know more? Or perhaps you've an urge to stretch yourself further. Then the Optional Extra pages are for you. They're optional. And they're ... yes, you get the idea.

They provide additional questions, topics and ideas and often lead to other related passages in the Bible. You'll find they zing home quite strongly what it all means for you and me.

Optional eXtra
Matthew 8-18
COR, CURE CARE

Chs. 8-9: 3 miracles (8 v1-17), break (v18-22), 3 more (8 v23 - 9 v8), break (9 v9-17), 3 more (v18-34), break (v35-38). You'll find almost all of these miracles recorded in the other gospels: Matthew's arranged them together, and more briefly.
• *What's the main point Matt's making about Jesus?*

v4: the command showed: a) Jesus' respect for the Old T; b) would officially restore the guy to society; c) would be a witness (or 'testimony') to the priests of Jesus' power. Old T regs on leprosy? Read Leviticus 13 v1-45, 14 v1-32.

v10-12: list the reasons why people today believe they should be OK with God and fit for heaven. What risk are they taking?
• *When it boils down to it, what are you relying on?*
• *Do your reasons begin 'Because I...' or 'Because Jesus...'?*

v11: heaven's like a feast. Great prospect, eh? Hell, v12, isn't. A constant awareness of being under God's punishment. Chew over the contrast. How will it make you pray?

NO COMPROMISE, PROMISE

v20: 'Son of Man': a title Jesus took from Psalm 8 & Daniel 7 v13-14, which talked of God's chosen, everlasting ruler.
• *What was Jesus saying about himself in passing?*

v21: maybe the guy's father had died already, or he was waiting for him to do so - so he could claim his inheritance.

We're not told how the two guys responded: Matthew wants us to concentrate on the radical demands of discipleship.

v22: was Jesus anti-family? Get real! No, he's merely saying that following him must always take top priority. See how sharply he put it in Luke 14 v25-35.
• *How important is Jesus to you?*
• *What's his message to those who aren't yet prepared to surrender to his rule? What's his message to those who want to postpone following him and keep him at arm's length?*

POWER POINT

Contrast Mark 4 v35 to 5 v20: Matthew's version has less detail - he wants to focus simply on Jesus' unique authority.

v27: in the Old T, it was the mark of God to control the weather. See Psalms 65 v5-8, 89 v8-9, 107 v23-32 and Job 38 v8-11.
9 v2-3: similarly, only God could pronounce forgiveness. Try Jeremiah 31 v34. What's all this saying about Jesus, then?

v29: 'the appointed time', ie God's final judgment. But in Jesus, that judgment had in part arrived. He did destroy the demons. And one day, he'll eradicate all evil finally.

v30-32: why the act of judgment on the pigs? We're not told if the Gadarenes (v28) were Jews or Gentiles: if Jews, they'd be breaking Old T regulations by keeping pigs.

9 v2: the Jews believed you got ill because you sinned. Jesus doesn't answer that here, but he does in John 9 v1-3.

Optional extra

A RIGHT MEAL OF IT

v9: see v1. Jesus was in Capernaum, his home town (4 v13). See the rise of opposition to Jesus: 9 v3, the teachers of the law attacked his teaching; v10, the Pharisees laid into his behaviour; v14, John the Bap's group (who had reason to mourn with J the B in prison, 4 v12) criticised his disciples.

v12: as 'doctor', what's Jesus' diagnosis? What's his cure?

v13: it's Hosea 6 v6: how dare God's people palm him off with religion, instead of putting their heart into serving him.
• *How do we fall into that same trap?*

v14: Jesus isn't anti-fasting. But remember Matt 6 v16-18?

v15: on Jesus as a bridegroom, see Matt 22 v1-14, 25 v1-13. On the church as his bride, see Revelation 19 v6-9.
• *When will the great 'wedding' take place?*
• *Are you getting prepared? How?*

MEAL-TIME, HEAL-TIME

Chs. 8-9 demonstrate... Jesus' unstoppable authority over the human body, nature and death; his total compassion for those regarded as second-rate; his mission and ability to deal with sin and forgive sinful men and women. Mind-blowing.

v21: for the regs on bleeding, see Leviticus 15 v25-27. Think how the woman shows a mix of superstition and faith.
• *Which is it that Jesus points to?*
Imagine her relief that Jesus accepted her - and healed her.
v27: 'son of David': the two were blind, but saw Jesus as the long-awaited Messiah, descended from king David, who was expected to restore sight to the blind: snatch Isaiah 35 v3-5.
• *How did Jesus do more than restoring physical sight?*

Does God do miracles now? Well, of course he *can*. But don't mis-read Matthew: these miracles were pointers to Jesus' identity, not models for our expectations today. But, hang on...
• *How is Jesus' cross and resurrection a great miracle?*
• *Doesn't God do miracles today? Doesn't he turn hard, self-centred individuals into people being re-made like Jesus? 'Can't change human nature'? Yes, that's a miracle of God.*

M PEOPLE

Ch. 10: the second teaching 'block' of Matt's gospel: the others being chs. 5-7, 13 v1-52, 18 and 24-25. Here Matt gathers different bits of Jesus' teaching into one chunk. Read it.

OK, what Jesus sends Christians to do now: Matt 28 v18-20.
• *What can Christians be sure of (v18, 20b)?*
• *What's our task (v19, 20a)? Who are we to go to (v19)?*
• *Does this describe you? How will you be more purposeful?*

9 v35: a re-cap as in 4 v23.
v36: Jesus as the 'Good Shepherd'? See John 10 v11-15.

v37: the harvest was an Old T picture of God's coming judgment: try Isaiah 27 v12, Hosea 6 v11, Joel 3 v13. So workers are needed to rescue people from God's judgment.
(cont)
• *What exactly are you doing about people's need and the*

Optional extra

big opportunity? What can you do straightaway (v38)?

10 v1: ah, twelve. Weren't there 12 tribes of Israel? Exactly! So here is God's 'new Israel', those who recognise Jesus.

v8b: 'freely give...' - as Jesus freely gave them his authority. The apostles were principally to preach and heal: think why Jesus didn't send them to teach about him at this stage.

v10-11: a clue on Christian work? Those who have such responsibilities (full or part-time) aren't to demand payment, but should be supported by those they help. See 1 Cor 9 v7-14.

v15: S and G were judged by God after refusing to listen to his messengers (Gen 19, esp v23-25). How much worse it would be for those who witnessed Jesus' authority first-hand.

TAKING THE TROUBLE

v16: shrewd as snakes, innocent as doves.
• *What's the danger of Christians being one but not the other?*
• *What should be our motives in our work for Jesus?*

v18 anticipates Jesus' later instructions (28 v19, Acts 1 v8).
v19: a promise for situations of extraordinary opposition. As seen with Paul in Acts 18 v12-17 & chs. 24-26. Read 'em!

v22: 'to the end', ie of our life or the persecution. Not *the* end.
v25: compare 9 v34.
v28: it's said: fear of people is self-interested cowardice, while fear of God is a healthy response of awe and obedience.

• *Which do you have?*
• *What's a worse fate than martyrdom, according to v28?*
• *What did you expect from the Christian life when you became a Christian? What do you now? Why?*

v29: '...apart from the will of your Father'. is literally 'without your Father'. ie, not even sparrows (poor people's food, then) die without God's knowledge. So v29-31 aren't saying God will rescue us from conflict (or even death) but he will care for us personally through it. We can't slip outside his care.

NO CON-CON CON

Bag Romans 10 v8-11: a ready, public acknowledgment of Jesus is an essential mark of discipleship. Agree? Is this you?

v34: Jesus *did* come to bring peace (see Luke 2 v14), just as the Messiah was predicted to (Isaiah 9 v6-7, Zec 9 v9-10). That peace (a restored rel with God) has begun, but not yet been completed (one day it will). So, for now, following the Prince of Peace brings conflict and division.
It's said: 'Home can be the hardest place to be a Christian.'
• *Have you, or friends of yours, found that? In what ways?*
• *How will stand for Jesus in your home and among your friends and also be a peace-maker there?*

v42: a cup of water: that was simple duty, then; 'little ones' = probably the 12; 'reward': as before in Matt, that's in heaven.

Optional eXtra

THE BAP CHAP

v2: maybe John's disciples were confused because they expected dramatic, immediate judgment (see 3 v11-12).

v5: Jesus is referring to an Old Testament prophecy which talked of the Messiah's role (bag Isaiah 35 v5-6, 61 v1).

v9-10, 14: see Malachi 3 v1, 4 v5-6.

v12: er, is difficult. It probably means Jesus' message has been making waves (boy, hadn't it!). 'Forceful men lay hold of it' could refer to John's arrest and imprisonment (4 v12).

v17: Jewish leaders had refused to celebrate with Jesus (like at a wedding) or repent at John's message (like at a funeral).
• *What outrageous assumptions had they drawn (v18-19)?*

Jot down all the wrong views of Jesus that you've heard.
• *How would you start to answer them?*
• *Why is it so important that we understand who Jesus is?*
'We need to understand who Jesus is if we're to respond to him as he wants'. Is that right?

RRRRRESPONSE

v21: on Tyre and Sidon's history, see Isaiah 23, Ezek 26-28.

v25: 'these things' presumably refers to the significance of Jesus' mission. Here, compare 1 Corinthians 1 v18-31.

v27: the relationship between God the Father and the Son.
• *What does it mean to 'know' God?*
• *How thankful are you for that relationship?*
• *What's the only way to come to know God?*

• *If spiritual understanding is the gift of God, how will you pray for your non-Christian friends?*

v28: catch an echo of Isaiah 55 here? Fantastic.
'Rest' doesn't mean an easy life: but it's relief from human religion (see Matt 23 v4), a rest from trying to be 'in' with God and the prospect of being part of God's rest (Heb 4 v1-11). It's 'easy' as it's serving him out of thanks, not obeying rules to try to be accepted. It's a 'yoke' as we submit to Jesus' rule.

v29: snatch Jeremiah 6 v16: now it's Jesus issuing the invite!

YEAH, AND THE REST

v8: when Jesus says he's Lord of the Sabbath, he means more than just that he decides what could happen on the Jewish day of rest. It also means he's in charge of heaven - where Christians will ultimately and fully enjoy God's rest. That's a double shock for the Pharisees: Jesus says he's God, the one in charge of the Sabbath. But he's also saying: 'If you want to get to heaven and know God's forgiveness, you need to come to me.' As he said just before (11 v28), right? If you didn't read it in the last OE, read Hebrew 4 v1-11. Ta.
• *How do we enjoy God's rest in part now?*

v3: that story of David is in 1 Samuel 21 v1-6.

• *How is Jesus greater than king David, greater than the temple, greater than the Old Testament?*

Optional etra

DRIVING TEST

v18-21: it's Isaiah 42 v1-4. Note Jesus' humility and refusal to complain (v19) and his gentleness (v20). See the reminder here of God's words at Jesus' baptism (3 v16-17).

v23: is this the 'Son of David', ie, the great liberator the people were waiting for? Explain their confusion, using v18-21.

v24: see v14. Sorcery was punishable by death.

v29: read Hebrews 2 v14-15.

v31-32: keep it in context. Speaking against Jesus could be forgiven, Jesus says, as he'd come in a way people didn't expect. But a perverse refusal to recognise such a healing (v22) as God's work was unforgivable. A difference between failing to recognise the truth - and a deliberate rejection of it. So, blasphemy against the Spirit now means refusing to recognise God's authority over us when we know that to be true. It's refusing to become a Christian, to submit to Jesus.

• Why is it that careless words v36 show our true character?
• Will you take v36 to heart, please?

REPEAT: REPENT

v38-39: see Luke 16 v30-31.
• Would another miracle have brought them to faith in God?
• What would you say to a friend who said 'If God could only prove he was there, I'd believe in him'?

Read the book of Jonah yet? Go on, won't take long. Catch the Queen of Sheba story in 1 KIngs 10 v1-13.

v39: adulterous: in jilting God for this sort of religion instead.

v41-42: take in 12 v6, too, and think again:
• How is Jesus greater than the temple (as a priest), greater than Jonah (as a prophet), greater than Solomon (as a king)? Enjoy Hebrews 4 v14-16 in this light.

v46: Joseph and Mary obviously had kids after Jesus' birth.

Giving Jesus a bit of attention at Christmas isn't discipleship.
• What will you do for your friends who think it's enough?

HEAR HERE

No, we're not mad, just a little cryptic (understand why?) Chew on each of the 'any ideas?' questions. Explanations next time!

HIDE AND SEED

• How does the parable mirror the events of chs. 11-12?

'The parable of the sower' is a duff title. Jesus doesn't explain much about the sower, seed, or harvest. We say: re-name it.

v11: remember 11 v25-27?

v18-22: isn't it incredible, given what people are like and all the distractions, that any respond? But some do! And there's a great crop for those keeping going with Jesus: others will become Christians. Hang in there. Keep praying for others.

Analyse your usual response to God's word.
• Are you in one of these four categories (v18-23)?
• What opposition and distractions will you deal with?

Optional e⌧tra

HANG ON FOR HARVEST

v24-30, 36-43: Jesus had announced God's kingdom (4 v17). Some would have thought they'd see a major disruption of society as a result. That's why Jesus tells this parable.

• *Instead, what were Jesus' disciples to expect?*

Ever think that the church seems unpromising, that the opposition is too strong, that there's little trust in God, that Christians are having zero influence, that it's all small-time stuff?

• *What great encouragement do these parables provide?*

v40-43: compare 8 v12, 25 v31-46.

v32: it's possible, given Daniel 4 v20-22, that the 'birds of the air' refers to the Gentile nations. Ah! Jesus' great mission.

v34: incredible, huh (remember v11)? Think why...

v43: only two results for people: punishment/anguish or acceptance/radiance (see Daniel 12 v3). Only then will it be obvious to all: those made 'righteous' by Jesus will 'shine'.

v43b: *NB! How will you take today's message to heart?*

WORTH MIRTH

v44: 'with joy': OK, so what happened to the excitement when you first became a Christian?

• *Is this true of you? How will you recapture that joy?*

Ask God. Perhaps apologise to him for forgetting how valuable it is to know him. Then let facts direct feelings: recall the incredible lengths God went to in order to rescue you from spending a self-obsessed life and eternity under his anger. Trusting that the cross of Jesus dealt with our sin opens a

friendship with God. In life now he forgives, challenges, assures, teaches, leads and re-makes us to be like his Son. One day, we'll share eternity *with God*.

• *Isn't that worth everything?*

Get a bite of Titus 3 v3-8 and Jude 24-25. And talk to God.

v52: refers back to v35, where Jesus' new teaching is identified as going back to the creation of the world. It's new and revolutionary, but firmly based on God's eternal truths.

• *What does this tell us about God and his plan for the world?*

HEADING OFF

v53: marks the end of the third chunk of teaching from Jesus in Matt's gospel (the first two being chs. 5-7 and 10). From 13 v53 - 17 v27, Matt closely follows Mark 6 v1 - 8 v30. Only he abbreviates more and includes some extra bits.

v54: on Naz, see 2 v23.

v54: his last recorded teaching in a synagogue. Think why.

v57: as we'll see later, people thought of Jesus as a prophet.

v58: his power wasn't magical or automatic. 8 v10, 13, yep?

14 v1: Herod was the son of big king Herod (2 v1, etc).

v12: make the link between John and Jesus' ministries. See 17 v12 (Elijah here = John). Jesus' messenger received the same opposition (and end result) that Jesus did.

• *Why do we kid ourselves it should be different for us?*

Ask God to help you stand firm in the face of opposition.

• *What forms does the opposition to your faith in Jesus take?*

Optional extra

BREAD ROLE

The feeding of the 5000 appears in all four gospels.

1. It shows Jesus creating: something only God can do.

2. It's a reminder: about God feeding his people in the desert (it's a remote place here, too, and everyone had enough). See Exodus 16 v1-18.

3. It's a pointer: that miracle in Exodus followed God rescuing his people from Egypt. God gave them bread from heaven so they'd remember being rescued (see Exodus 16 v32-34). So... when Jesus fed the 5000 with bread from heaven, it would have raised questions: what's Jesus' rescue? When will it happen? How will it be like God's rescue in Exodus? The Jews wrongly assumed it was going to be a rescue from Roman domination. No! Wait for what Jesus says in Matt 16. Read John 6 for Jesus' teaching on the miracle's significance. It's incredible what he says it shows about himself (v33-35).

v25: 'fourth watch':, ie between 3am and 6am.

v28-31: a rush of blood to Peter's brain... but the lesson's clear: trust isn't sitting back hoping things will work out, but it's an active, ongoing reliance on God's promises.

• *In what situations do you need to start trusting him?*

COME CLEAN

v2: 'tradition of the elders': a load of rules passed down by word of mouth (only later written down). The Pharisees' big mistake? Making these equal in authority with the Old T.

v6: contrast with 5 v17 - Jesus' attitude and mission.

v5: see the Pharisees' sidestep? 'Sorry, Mum, no birthday present - I promised it to God instead.' Despicable.

Think of some of the ways we're tempted to make being fit for God a matter of rules and regulations.

• *How are we in danger of letting tradition have an equal authority with God's word? Think of a) yourself b) your church.*

v19: Jesus isn't saying we can't be creative, logical, etc. He's saying that when it comes to being fit for God our hearts ('what makes us tick') are totally debased. We need new hearts. The heart of the human problem is the problem of the human heart.

• *Didn't Jesus have something to say about this in John 3?*

BREAD? CRUMBS...

v21: T & S last got mentioned by Jesus in 11 v22.

v23: the disciples' request (as Jesus' answer indicates) means: 'Go on Jesus, do yer miracle and send her off.' His reply (see 10 v5-6) tests her faith. She came back to Jesus.

v26: a teasing answer, based on the Jewish view of Gentiles as 'dogs'. The woman replies (v27): 'Well, in that case, at least let the dogs have the dogs' rations!'

• *What had she understood that the disciples hadn't?*

• *Remember 28 v18-20?*

Basket case: the word used in 14 v20 describes a hand-basket as used by Jews. The different word in 15 v37 is a more general purpose basket as used by non-Jews. A minor detail, but it shows Matt's care to show these are Gentiles. Smart!

Optional eXtra

SIGN LANGUAGE

v1: the Pharisees were the ultra-religious group who knocked up loads of extra rules to living for God; the Sadduccees were a well-to-do sect who held there was no life after death. The Phars and the Sads were enemies - opposed to each other's teaching - yet here, ironically, united in their hatred of Jesus.

v4: as we've read before in 12 v38-42.

v8-11: the disciples' double mistake was: a) failing to trust Jesus for food b) failing to grasp his teaching.
• *v9-10: how do you need to learn the lesson of 6 v25-34?*

v12: *how carefully do you listen to 'Bible teaching'?*
• *What teaching around today do we need to guard against?*

Spot the counterfeits: how to judge Bible teachers we hear. Think Bible, Gospel and Jesus. Try asking: do they believe...
... Jesus was 100% God, 100% man? ... in God as Trinity? ... in the Bible? ... in sin? ... in Jesus' death?   Don't hold back!

IN THE PICTURE

v13: Caesarea Philippi... isn't it a tad ironic that Peter's great confession should come in non-Jewish territory?
v16: 'living God' - in contrast with all the local, useless idols.

v14: the Jews thought Elijah would return (see Malachi 4 v5); Herod (see Matt 14 v2) thought Jesus was John the Bap back from the dead. Jesus was likened to Jeremiah as he was a prophet of judgment, rejected by the people.
v18: clever play of words: Peter means rock. On him - the trusting, faithful, obedient Peter - Jesus will build his church. Try some of Peter's sermons at the start of Acts. Top stuff! Snatch also Ephesians 2 v19-21.
• *Whose church is it, by the way (Matt 16 v18)?*

v19: 'bind' here probably = 'forbid', 'loose' prob. = 'permit', ie Peter's authority is not to do with admission to the 'kingdom' (that's Jesus' job) but teaching and organising its members. See Peter do that in Acts 15 v7-11 (based on chs. 10-11).

• *v15: why is Jesus' question still significant for everybody?*

DEATH ROW?

v21: 'from that time on', ie only now could he start to explain what sort of Messiah he was. See who'd punish him too: it'd be an official execution, ordered by the Jewish ruling council, people who supposedly knew God and their Old Testaments.

v27: Jesus' future role. Think what he knows about us.

v28: hard to tell if this is referring to the transfiguration (that's next in Matt's gospel) or the resurrection, or Pentecost or the telling of the good news of Jesus' rule. Any ideas?

Using v13-28, imagine explaining to a non-Christian friend: a) who Jesus is; b) what he came to do c) what response he demands. Why not practise what you would say?
• *How will you now pray for them on the lines of v17?*

Optional eXtra

CLOUD 'N' CROWD

v1: in the Old T, Moses went up a mountain to meet God. (Exodus 24 v9-18, 31 v18). Elijah, too (1 Kings 19 v8-18).

v5: It's Jesus that God singles out here: his Son, who fulfils all the law and the prophets. Hebrews 1 v1-4, right?

v14: interestingly, Moses too returned to a scene of spiritual crisis (Exodus 32) - just as Jesus did here.

v5: heard that somewhere before? 3 v17 perhaps?
• *How would the transfiguration have helped the disciples?*
• *How would it have helped Jesus?*

v10: the Jews believed (based on Malachi 4 v5) that Elijah would return before the arrival of God himself. Jesus says he has: John the Bap was that Elijah.

Can we expect visions of Jesus, direct words from God, too?
• *Doesn't the Bible give us that vision and God's direct words?*
Read John 20 v24-31. Note especially v29 and 31.

NO KIDDING

v3: of course, lurches us towards John 3 v3, naturally.

v3-5: the context (17 v24-27, 18 v1) shows Jesus is talking about having the status of children, not their particular qualities (receptiveness, trustfulness etc). Right?

v4: 'humbles himself': the same word is used of Jesus in Philippians 2 v8 (see v5-11): God made himself nothing.
• *How should this motivate you? Does it?*

v7: Jesus recognises: a) the world is full of things that cause people to sin; b) people are individually responsible.

• *How is Jesus both realistic and challenging?*

v10: angel delight! We've always personal access to God.

v12-14: contrast Luke 15 v1-7, where it's probably spoken on a different occasion. See who Jesus was talking to (Lk 15 v2) and the point made (Lk 15 v7). Clever use of the same story!

• *How serious are you about stuff that causes you to sin and about what you do (or fail to do) that makes others sin?*
• *Need to make an action plan?*
• *Need to ask an older Christian to keep an eye on you?*

FORGIVE AND REGRET?

v18: used before of Peter (16 v19). Now that authority is invested in the local church. No more details given here!

v19-20: presumably the two or three were meeting to pray for the wrongdoer, but the principle goes wider: where a handful of Christians gather in Jesus' name (to do his purpose), agree and pray, then he is with them. And God will answer!
• *How does this transform your small Christian gatherings?*

v21: see Genesis 4 v24. Just as Lamech's revenge was unlimited, get the contrast? So should our forgiveness be.
• *What evidence is there that you know God's forgiveness?*
• *Do you care for others' walk with God? Are you quick to apologise to others? Do you forgive? Need to ask God's help?*

Optional e🅇tra

JOB

NOW

There's lots we don't know about Job: when and where it was written, where the story took place and who wrote it, etc. But it has universal, timeless relevance in the face of a common human experience - suffering. Worth a good look, we feel.

v1: Job was blameless, not perfect. Hence the sacrifices (v5).

v6-12: 'Satan' means 'accuser.' What are we to make of him? Some people get wrongly worked up about him, others don't take him seriously enough. Here (v7), we're not told where he comes from, but he's testing the loyalty of God's people. Now see v9-12: his power is limited. He's on a chain. Never think that God and Satan are two equal powers fighting over the universe. No way. God alone is in charge.
The New T tells us that Jesus has broken the devil's power.
Tuck into Hebrews 2 v14-15 and 1 John 3 v8.
Essentially the devil's power is that of lies - including making people believe that he's more powerful than he really is.
• How encouraging are James 4 v7 and 1 Peter 5 v8-9?

Angels? Hebrews 1 v14 is good!

POW

1 v21: compare 1 Timothy 6 v7-8.
2 v8: contrast with what Job was (1 v3b).

In the Lord's Prayer, we say: 'Your will be done.'
• Could we say the same in Job's situation?

• Do you mean those words when you say them?
Are you prepared for times of trouble? The New T is full of warnings that the way of Jesus is the way of suffering.
• Why do we keep expecting otherwise?
See how Romans 8 v18-39 brings suffering and hope together.

Heard it said: 'I can't believe in God in a world of suffering'? Well, consider the alternative: if there's no God, then suffering and disasters are mere random accidents. There would never be any answers. LIfe would be down to chance, it would be crushingly pointless. But if you're making that statement above, aren't you saying there must be answers somewhere? The Bible maintains God gives answers, a right perspective. (More details in a later Optional Extra).
• What do you think God's perspective on suffering will be?

OW

4 v12-16: Eliphaz makes his vision a yardstick by which to judge others' relationship with God. Dangerous... we should thank God for our experience of him, but be careful not to make that experience compulsory for others.
• Can you think of an example of this you've come across?

Fill in the gaps: perhaps you'd like to read all of Job in ch. 3.

See God's view of the friends' advice in ch. 42 v7-8.

5 v17: compare Psalm 94 v12, Hebrews 12 v5-11.
• Is God's discipline a mark of his anger or love?
• Are you co-operating with God, or reacting against him?

Optional extra

ROW

Chs. 8-31: heaps to read here. Perhaps you could do so one speech at a go some time.

Ch. 28, on wisdom, is one of the gems of the Bible. Enjoy it! It fits together like this: v1-11: humanity is clever; v12: but it can't find wisdom; v13-19: wisdom can't be bought or sought; **v20**: where is wisdom?; v21-27: true wisdom is God's gift; **v28**: what true wisdom is. Cracking words.

23 v2-3, 29 v2-5: Job desired a restored relationship with God. In the whole book, he never once asked for his body to be healed, or his property and goods to be restored.
But take note how acutely he suffered in body, mind and soul: (10 v8-9,16v7-9, 30 v20-23). Which was his worst suffering?
• *What sort of example is he in this to us?*

But see Job's growing bitterness: he wants answers from God, as in 10 v2, 13 v3, 23 v4-7, 31 v35-37. More on this later!

• *How does 9 v33 point us to Jesus?*

YOW

34 v5-6 is a mis-quote. Eilhu has misrepresented God. You won't find the words of v5b and 6a in Job's speeches.

35 v9-16: Elihu is wrong to suggest that God only hears when our motives are totally pure or when there's no sin in our hearts. If that was so, no-one could know God's rescue.
• *How does Mark 9 v24 help us here?*

Ch. 37, the end of Elihu's speech is a right stormer. Enjoy! v13 shows both the kindness and severity of God, right? Think of another day when the sky was dark, and an innocent man suffered (see Mark 15 v33-41).
• *How did that event show both God's anger and his love?*

Famous quote from an author called C S Lewis:
'God whispers to us in our pleasures, speaks to us in our consciences and shouts to us in our pain. Pain is his megaphone to rouse a deaf world.'
• *How was that true for Job?*
• *How do you react to the quote?*

HOW

God didn't charge Job with sin or rebuke him for maintaining his integrity. But see what he says in 38 v2 and 40 v2. Job had pleaded for an interview with God in which his innocence could be established. In reply, God proves Job's littleness.
• *Why do you think Job is answered like this?*

Think whether Job's real problem was his physical suffering or his suffering in relation to God.
• *So how would hearing what God said have helped him?*

'God didn't answer Job's questions, but the need of his heart.'
• *Agree/disagree?*

• *What does God's creation tell us about him?*

• *What response should this produce in us?*

Optional e❌tra

BOW

v1-6: Job has been given no explanation of his sufferings.
• *What brought him to the real humility he showed here?*

Get it right: Job didn't repent 'cos he knew good things might come his way as a result. No. He just did what was right. But v10-17 are intriguing: was this a *reward* from God? Well... remember 1 v21, 2 v10? So this kindness here is God's grace, it's undeserved generosity. But think also... Jesus did speak of rewards for those who serve him well (Matt 5 v11-12). Those rewards will be fully ours in heaven. But we're to serve God for who he is, not for the motive of reward, right?

The first temptation (Genesis 3) was that we could do a better job than God, that we should be in his place. Remember God's ironic words to Job in 40 v8-14? In ch. 42, Job - rightly - totally rejects such thoughts.

v7-8: 'my servant' points to the suffering servant of Isaiah 53.
• *And how does Psalm 73 add to our understanding of Job?*

After ch. 2, Satan isn't mentioned. It's God who's important.

There's lots we've left unread in Job. Come back to it soon!

v7: Job's friends would certainly have agreed with what God had said to Job. But God was angry with them. Why? Job had quarrelled with God, doubted his justice, insisted on his own innocence, even wanted to end his life. Yet God said he'd spoken what was right. Why?

VOW

Job learns that he won't always find answers to life's deepest problems. But he is brought to recognise that God is totally in control of his world and loves and cares for him - even when he can't understand what on earth is going on.
Romans 8 v28-29 is worth another read: list all the things that Christians can be sure about this side of heaven.

It's been said: 'When we cannot trace God's hand, we can trust his heart.' Right? How have we seen Job do this?

Just so you know: Job is mentioned in Ezekiel 14 v14 and James 5 v11 and quoted in 1 Corinthians 3 v19. Mmm, really.

Job had knowledge of God through creation. We have it through redemption (what Jesus achieved). Job had knowledge of God through crocodiles. We have it through the cross.
• *How much more do we know about God than Job?*
• *How must this help us in hard times?*
• *How is talking about the cross pretty much essential when people say: 'I can't believe in God in a world of suffering'?*

On God's wisdom, slip into 1 Corinthians 1 & 2 sometime.

'The Bible has no unqualified promise that God will heal us from illness.' Is that right? Then, so what?

Last thing: be thankful. John Calvin (theologian, died 1564) preached 159 sermons on Job. You've only had nine studies!

Optional e⌧tra
I TIMOTHY
FALSE START

Read Paul's earlier warning in Acts 20 v13-38 (esp v28-31).

v3: the tone of it suggests Timothy needed a kick into action.

• *Why is it always worth fighting for the truth of the Bible?*

v8-10: the list has the same order as the Ten Commandments (Exodus 20 v1-17). This law should restrain and convict evil-doers - and point them to the gospel.

• *How is the gospel the answer to 'the law'?*

• *Does v5 sum up you, your motives, your action to others?*

• *What false teachings are popular but dangerous today?*
Then think how to answer those who believe or teach them.
Think how you'd talk about Jesus to someone from one of the sects (Jehovah's Witnesses, Mormons, Moonies etc).

'It doesn't matter if Jesus really rose from the grave as long as he's alive in my heart.' Go on, why is that wrong?

MINUTE STEAK

See Acts 8 v1-3,9 v1-31: Paul's conversion, before and after.

Many people often feel guilty about all the things they've done in the past. How does this passage help them?

v12: like Paul, those trusting Jesus' rescue are to serve him.

• *Or are you all 'take' from God and no 'give'?*

• *In what specific way will you serve him better from now on?*

v15: Paul doesn't say '...of whom I *was* the worst', but 'I *am*'.

• *How does this encourage Christians who always feel they're never good enough to be used by God?*

• *How does it challenge those who look down on others?*

• *What does it tell us about the ongoing Christian life?*

v17: the God of this gospel is the sovereign ruler, immune to decay, unobservable to human eyes and the one true God. All together now: to him be glory and honour for ever. Amen!

v18: 'prophecies': ie, words spoken about Timothy's task.

v20: compare 1 Cor 5 v5. H is named also in 2 Tim 2 v17-18.

PRAYER TONIC

Six reasons to pray like this? We reckon they're comme ça:

1. God likes it - he's a rescuing God (v3-4).

2. There's only one God (v5a), dealing the same way with all.

3. There's only one way to God - thru' Jesus (v5b).

4. His death was on everyone's behalf (v6a).

5. The cross demonstrated God's purpose (v6b).

6. Paul's call from God was to Gentiles, too (v7).

Requests, prayers, intercession, thanks (v1).

• *Can you define the possible content of each of these?*

• *How is your church at prayer? How can you encourage it?*

v2: peace-time is an advantage - it allows Christians to concentrate on telling others the gospel, as God wants (v3).

• *Which friends do you need to get back praying for? Go on!*

Optional eXtra

ADDRESSING THE ADDRESS

This passage gets used to answer a handbagful of questions about feminism and women's roles - whereas in fact, Paul was addressing a specific problem: the teaching role in church. Keep the verse in its context.

Other helpful passages on women's ministry are 1 Corinthians 11 v2-16, 14 v26-39. Titus 2 v3-4. See also Acts 18 v24-26. There are great, and vital, teaching opportunities for women.

v13: Paul doesn't put the blame entirely on Eve for the fall (Genesis 3). In Romans 5, the responsibility for it is Adam's. Eve was deceived, Adam disobeyed God's order knowingly.

v15: presumably to be taken with Genesis 3 v16: God's curse on Eve was shown by pain in childbirth. Now Jesus has in his death taken God's curse away. Although its effects remain (sin, pain in childbirth etc are still with us), we know the curse is removed - so we can be rescued by God. And the way to salvation? See v15b: faith, love, holiness. True for all, right? Get talking with others: 1 Tim 2 needs discussing!

LEADING QUESTION

v2, 4: should all church leaders be married with kids, then? No. It says 'husband of *but* one wife' ie, just the one - a one-woman man. So the principle here is that he's got to be godly. Polygamy would show clearly that he wasn't.

v2-3: all these are general Christian qualities, apart from one.
• *Which is it?*

Cracked it? He must be 'able to teach' (from the Bible).
• *What does this tell us about the prime job of a church leader?*
Think (from ch. 1) why this was so vital in Ephesus.

• *What qualities would you look for in a Christian leader?*
• *What qualities do we (wrongly) tend to look for first?*

Compare Paul's instructions to Titus (Ti 1 v5-9, 2 v1-15).
• *If you were starting a church from scratch, what jobs and duties would you give to people?*

v11: how can the church use women's ministries without falling into gender stereotyping (eg women make the teas, etc)?

BODY OF TRUTH?

v1: 'The Spirit says...' Maybe Paul was talking about an Old T prophecy, or something God had directly revealed to him as an apostle. As in Acts 20 v23 and 21 v11.

v1, v6: 'the faith': by this time there was a recognised content to Christian truth. It could be used to judge false teachers.
• *How much do you analyse teaching or advice you receive to check if it's biblical or not?*

v3: know the Bible's view on marriage? And on foods? Sure?
• *How much do you enjoy and thank God for everything?*

• *What place is there in the Christian life for sport/leisure (v8)?*
• *Why is it to be enjoyed (v4)? What about yourself in this?*

Optional extra

LEADING ARTICLE

v12: Tim might have been anything up to the age of 35 - but:
* *What can young people do for God that older Christians are less able to do?*

v13-16: God's gifts require our co-operation (v14). Tim was to exercise his spiritual gifts and abilities as best as he could.
* *How will you serve God with what he's given you?*

v16: a great motto. As Christians we should ensure our life-style and beliefs measure up to what Jesus requires of us.
* *What areas of Christian lifestyle are hard for young people?*
* *What Christian beliefs do you find it difficult to hold on to?*

v9: the third 'trustworthy saying' in 1 Tim. Memorizing them?

v10: the Bible says God cares for all (eg, Matt 5 v45) - but it's only Christians who'll know the depth of his care, which he has shown in Jesus Christ's death on our behalf.
Our God is living (v10). Forgotten that?

WIDOW WINDOW

* *What will it mean to you in practice to heed v 1-2?*
* *Why is the model of the family a helpful one to describe the local church?*

v8: 'worse than an unbeliever': ie, even the non-Christian recognises his duty to care for his elderly relatives. Do we?

v12: those younger widows stood self-condemned. They were using widowhood as a chance to be talkative busybodies rather than active workers, serving Jesus. In that situation, re-marriage would give them a better focus (v14).
* *What principles do you think underlie Paul's advice here?*

Read Acts 6 v1-7, 11 v19-30.
* *What's taught here about the church's responsibilities?*

Think about the different age groups in your church, or especially needy people. Pray for those in need.

ALL ABOUT WORTHING

v17: 'worthy of double honour': ie these leaders should be both fully respected and supported financially

v18: quotes from Deut 25 v4 (meaning 'don't stop the ox from having a bit to eat while it's working) and Luke 10 v7. Both are called Scripture, God's authoritative word. Think how this tiny reference can strengthen our trust in all of the Bible.

v22: Tim wasn't to make hasty appointments or he might end up in compromise himself. See the command for him (v22b)?
v23: nice personal touch from Paul, in line with 3 v3a.

See Paul's other teaching on slavery: Ephesians 6 v5-9, Colossians 3 v22 - 4 v1, Philemon, 1 Corinthians 7 v20-24.

* *How will you pray for your Christian leaders from now on?*
* *How will you go about your work from now on?*

Optional extra

MONEY-CHANGER

v3: what's always the benchmark for judging true teaching? Of course! You can spot a counterfeit £10 note by holding it up to the light. Same principle when you come across teaching you're not sure about. Ask: does it square with the Bible?

• *What's 'prosperity teaching' or the 'health & wealth' gospel? How should we answer it?*

• *Are you a 'trendy' Christian (always jumping on the latest 'Christian' idea or bandwagon) or a 'Bible' Christian?*

'Money is the root of all kinds of evil.' Right or wrong (v10)?

• *How is that a helpful distinction to make? Is God anti-money?*

v9: those who want to get rich get enticed, ensnared, obsessed and overwhelmed by it. Serious warnings here.

• *How should the Christian's attitude to money and possessions differ from everybody else's?*

Read more of Paul's attitude in Philippians 4 v10-13.

• *Do you share his contentment irrespective of circumstances?*

TACKLING TACTICS

Go back over 1 Tim and work out what its main themes have been under sorting the church out: eg, the need for proper Bible-teaching in the church. Choose at least two others! Then thank God for everything you've learnt from 1 Tim.

• *To recommend it to a friend, what would you say?*

v12: it's fantastic, isn't it? Chew over what 'take hold of the eternal life' means. Then get up, get on and live it.

v12: how can it help to give a public testimony to our faith?

• *If you know you're a Christian, how can you make your faith in Jesus more publicly known?*

v17-18: what we've got, we're to enjoy (and thank God for it - remember 4 v3-4?) and share with others. Do you do that?

v13: the ultimate reason why we must persevere is because Jesus persevered. He did so to the very end - even before Pilate when an opportunity came to deny everything, walk free and escape the cross. Thank God, Jesus didn't walk away. On Jesus and Pilate, read John 18 v28 - 19 v16.

• *Are you set to stick with Jesus in the long run?*

the ichthus file

The Bible fair and square

The Ichthus File No 8: Matthew 8-18; Job; I Timothy

© St Matthias Press/Radstock Ministries 1996

St Matthias Press

P.O.Box 665, London SW20 8RU England

Tel: (0181) 947 5686 Fax: (0181) 944 7091

Radstock Ministries

2a Argyle Street Mexborough South Yorkshire S64 9BW

Tel: (01709) 582345 Fax: (01709) 583202

Registered Charity 326 879

ISBN 1 873166 24 9

The Ichthus File was brought to you by:

Editor: Al Horn

Publisher: Tim Thornborough

Project chairman: Steve Timmis

Project manager: Ian Bull

Picky Pic Picker of the month: Tim Morton

Contributors of the month award:

Nic Roach, Al Horn. And a thumping great handshake of thanks to Doug Johnson.

Dilemma of the moment:

What do you do if you spill cherry yogurt down your keyboard? Answer: stick to peach melba.

What else are you looking for here? This is just the back page! If you want food, go and buy a Big Muck. If you want a laugh, go and look in the mirror. If you want a year's subscription, ring St Matthias Press. If you want fashion advice, don't call us. We'll call you. If you want entertainment, buy a carton of orange juice and stare in hushed wonder and awe at the word 'concentrate.'

Cheers!